Perfect Phrases for Real Estate Agents and Brokers

Also available from McGraw-Hill

Perfect Phrases for Performance Reviews by Douglas Max and Robert Bacal

Perfect Phrases for Performance Goals by Douglas Max and Robert Bacal

Perfect Solutions for Difficult Employee Situations by Sid Kemp

Perfect Phrases for Customer Service by Robert Bacal

Perfect Phrases for Business Proposals and Business Plans by Don Debelak

Perfect Phrases for Meetings by Don Debelak

Perfect Phrases for the Sales Call by William T. Brooks

Perfect Phrases for Lead Generation by William T. Brooks

Perfect Phrases for Sales and Marketing by Barry Callen

Perfect Phrases for Executive Presentations by Alan Perlman

Perfect Phrases for College Application Essays by Sheila Bender

Perfect Phrases for Writing Grant Proposals by Beverly Browning

Perfect Phrases for Real Estate Agents and Brokers

Dan Hamilton

New York Chicago San Francisco Lisbon
London Madrid Mexico City Milan New Delhi
San Juan Seoul Singapore Sydney Toronto

The **McGraw·Hill** Companies

Copyright © 2009 by The McGraw-Hill Companies, Inc. Printed in the United States of America. Except as permitted under the United States Copyright Act of 1976, no part of this publication may be reproduced or distributed in any form or by any means, or stored in a database or retrieval system, without the prior written permission of the publisher.

This is a *CWL Publishing Enterprises Book* produced for McGraw-Hill by CWL Publishing Enterprises, Inc., Madison, Wisconsin, www.cwlpub.com.

1 2 3 4 5 6 7 8 9 0 DOC/DOC 0 1 0 9 8

ISBN 13: 978-0-07-158835-5
MHID: 0-07-158835-3

McGraw-Hill books are available at special quantity discounts to use as premiums and sales promotions, or for use in corporate training programs. To contact a representative, please visit the Contact Us pages at www.mhprofessional.com.

Contents

Contents

Contents

Contents

Contents

Preface

Perfect Phrases for Real Estate Agents and Brokers is designed and written to provide real estate professional salespeople dialogues to help them build their careers. Real estate as an industry is hungry for better and more effective dialogues to raise the quality of service rendered to the community. The "perfect phrases" in this book will allow real estate professionals to demonstrate their value and worth to their clients and will give them the personal power to succeed.

After reading this book, you should be able to recognize the need to ask lots of questions. The trick to handling any objection is to ask lots of questions. The secret to closing more sales is asking lots of questions. The talent in landing an appointment is asking lots of questions. The ability to ask the questions can be developed only with the proper dialogues and though a great deal of practice.

Chapter 1 deals with the proper way to handle incoming calls. The dialogues are designed to create appointments that create sales that create income. Chapters 2 through 5 are prospecting chapters. The dialogues in these chapters are designed to discover those individuals who are interested in selling real estate. Prospecting using the proper dialogues is the most important function of the professional real estate salesperson. Without leads the professional has nothing except empty time, and in real estate time is money and should not be wasted.

Chapter 6 is written for the listing appointment. The dialogues will lead a homeowner to list with you, an outcome that benefits both parties. The chapter also includes dialogues developed to aid in the marketing and the eventual sale of the property.

Chapter 7 is intended for working with the buyers of real estate. Included in the chapter are the dialogues necessary to take a buyer from day one through to closing. Buyers who are not handled properly can be a huge source of irritation and a killer of time for the real estate professional.

The last chapter, Chapter 8, is probably the most important. It gives you the proper dialogues to handle objections and the proper dialogues to close a transaction. Those professionals who can help others make a commitment are the ones who succeed.

The book is written in conversational English such as would be used in everyday real estate business. Each situation presented is one that occurs frequently in the business. No filler or fluff here, just straight-to-the-point dialogues.

You should read through the entire book first and then study the sections that are relevant to what you are experiencing. Once you are thoroughly versed in the dialogues, you should use the book as a resource.

Acknowledgments

When I was selected to write this book, I was honored because I feel that "perfect phrases" dialogues are one of the most important assets of a successful real estate professional. Being able to use the proper dialogues will enable a real estate salesperson to make a fine living. To be invited to write this book is not only an honor but also a responsibility. The responsibility is to give the readers of this book the most appropriate dialogues for the most common situations in real estate. To give the readers every dialogue for every possible situation would be impossible, and the effort would result in a book thousands of pages long and hence of no real use.

I also feel honored in being asked to author this book because I am now part of a series of successful books that help people in all walks of life. This is a legacy that I will always look upon with gratitude.

I would first like to thank John Woods and his associates with CWL Publishing Enterprises for believing in me enough as an author that he selected me for this project. I hope I have met and exceeded your expectations.

Thanks to my wife, Kimberly, and daughter, Brittany. Both are my inspirations and have taught me so much about divine, unconditional, agape love. Thanks to the other members of my family, who have been with me throughout my real estate career.

And thanks to you, for buying and reading this book. Without you none of this is possible. I hope I will meet and exceed your expectations also.

About the Author

Dan Hamilton is an investor in single-family residential real estate property, the director of training for Century 21 Judge Fite Company, the director of career development for Century 21 Judge Fite Company, the operations manager for Real Estate Career Training school, lead trainer for Real Estate Career Training and Century 21 Judge Fite organization, a recruiter for Century 21 Judge Fite Company, president and founder of InveSTAR's real estate investment group, and a member of the Business Administration Advisory Committee for Tarrant County College District.

He is the author of *Real Estate Marketing and Sales Essentials: Steps for Success* and *Real Estate Brokerage: A Guide to Success*. Both of these books have been approved for the "Salespersons Annual Education" credit courses by TREC, and both have been picked up by Thompson-Southwestern Publishing to be distributed internationally.

Hamilton was consistently the top producer of his real estate office as well as a certified relocation specialist, a new agent trainer, a member of the Multi-Million Dollar Club, and a regional multiple award winner. He was twice awarded the regional Superstar designation.

He is a member of the National Association of Realtors, Texas Real Estate Teachers Association, Texas Association of Realtors, Real Estate Educators Association, and Greater Arlington Association of Realtors. He has the Graduate Realtor Institute designation and the Instructor Training Institute designation.

Chapter 1
Telephone Dialogues

P eople in the real estate industry have been far behind in the ability to answer the telephone and then convert those calls into money. This chapter is intended to overcome this deficit and move the industry forward in professionalism and service. Failure to use telephone dialogues effectively will greatly hinder a real estate company.

This chapter presents and discusses the following:

- Dialogues for answering the telephone correctly
- Dialogues for answering the telephone while taking opportunity time
- Generic dialogues for answering calls from buyers
- Specific dialogues for answering calls from buyers

This chapter is intended for practically anyone in the real estate business. It is specifically of benefit to salespeople, brokers, managers, attorneys, accountants, other real estate professionals, lending professionals, real estate investors, and title officers. All of the above will benefit from knowing about the telephone dialogues discussed in this chapter. Without this knowledge, these people in the real estate business are disadvantaged.

These are the objectives of this chapter:

- Understand the objective of the broker when advertising.
- Understand the objective of the agent when answering the telephone.
- Understand the objective of the caller when calling about a real estate advertisement.
- Understand the three things that buyers feel are of value.
- Understand the rules of handling calls from buyers.
- Understand and use the dialogues given for handling calls from buyers.

Answering the Telephone Correctly

Answering the telephone correctly in the real estate office is of utmost importance. A real estate company must make every effort to remain a professional organization. A key element of that image is answering the telephone professionally.

Most offices have an administrative assistant, receptionist, or call coordinator to answer the telephone. However, on certain occasions, you—the real estate professional—may need to answer that telephone.

Whoever answers the telephone should say:

"Thank you for calling Acme Real Estate Company. May I help you?"

This allows the caller to give his or her reason for calling. If the call is for another person in the office, then the person answering should forward the call. If the other person is not currently in the office, the person answering the call should say:

"Bob is not answering his page, but I would be glad to transfer you to his voice mail."

Then the person answering the call should transfer the call to voice mail. If the caller does not want to be connected to voice mail, the person answering the call should take his or her name and number and place them in voice mail.

The person answering the call should never say any of the following to a caller:

"Bob hasn't made it into the office yet."

"Bob is off on Thursday."

"I haven't seen Bob in days."

Answering the Telephone During Opportunity Time

Opportunity time is the time when a real estate agent gets the opportunity to take incoming calls from potential buyers. Opportunity time is also misnamed "floor time" and "up time," but make no mistake—if this time is handled properly, then it's an opportunity.

You should prepare for opportunity time as you would prepare for any other important task. Prior to opportunity time, you should do the following:

- Block out that time without any interruptions or appointments.
- Know and preview all the in-house inventory.
- Know each current print (newspaper and magazine) advertisement for real estate and have copies of those ads.
- Have a list of alternative properties.
- Adjust your attitude for the prospect of doing business, not the belief that it's a waste of time.

While on opportunity time, you should always be prepared to receive calls. If the agent on opportunity time is allowed to do paperwork while receiving calls, then you should have that work at hand. You should never be running around the office gathering things to do while on opportunity time.

You should have dialogues posted above your telephone for quick access if an opportunity call comes in. You should always be prepared to discontinue any current activities if a call comes in. Failure to take an incoming opportunity call seriously is costly.

Answering the Telephone with the Correct Attitude

Before answering an opportunity call, you should smile and smile big. Callers can pick up on the mood of the person answering their call. Have you ever called a business and been answered by a person who snapped at you? How did you feel? Did you want to give the company your business? Have you ever called a business and been answered by a person who made you feel welcome and wanted? There's a big difference—and all because of the tone of voice and inflection of the person answering the call. For each call, imagine that the caller has a check for several thousand dollars and all you have to do is convince him or her to put your name on it. That should make a difference in your attitude.

Objective of the Broker When Advertising

The objective of a broker in running any type of advertising is simply to make the telephone ring. The broker cannot expect to get buyers without making the telephone ring in the real estate office. If buyers are calling, then the broker has done his or her job.

Objective of the Agent When Answering the Telephone

The objective of the agent when answering the telephone is simply to make an appointment. No other objective should ever enter the situation. Some real estate salespeople try and sell a property over the telephone. Newsflash—it can't be done! The buyer always wants to see the property first. Anyway, the buyer cannot reach through the telephone lines and sign a contract. So don't try to sell a property over the telephone. Set an appointment to meet at the office!

Here are two things about getting the buyer to agree to an appointment:

The first thing is to ensure that the buyer likes you and trusts you. You can never set an appointment with a buyer or any client without those positive feelings. Give buyers a little TLC:

They have to	**T — Trust**	you,
They have to	**L — Like**	you,
Before you can ever	**C — Close.**	

Getting buyers to like you and trust you is relatively easy—as long as you make them feel comfortable with you and you don't sound like a "pushy" salesperson.

The second thing is to give the buyer something of value. The three things that buyers feel are of value are:

- Savings of money
- Savings of time
- Convenience of working with you

If you demonstrate your professionalism and offer your services in the manner prescribed in the following paragraphs, you will find that buyers will like you, they will trust you, and you can get them into your office because you have shown them something of value—something that other real estate agents have failed to do.

Objective of the Caller When Calling on a Real Estate Advertisement

The objective of the caller when calling on a real estate advertisement is simply to eliminate that ad. Buyers will circle multiple ads and have no intention of seeing all the properties. So they will call the real estate office and determine if they want to eliminate that ad. There's a problem: when they eliminate that ad, they also eliminate you!

Rules for Handling a Buyer Call

To repeat, the objective of a buyer is to eliminate the ad. Since we know that, our job is to prevent elimination and get the appointment.

Rule 1: Never try to sell the house the buyer called about.
Rule 2: Whoever asks the questions has control of the conversation.
Rule 3: If the buyer asks a question, he or she deserves an answer.
Rule 4: If you answer a question, always follow up with a question of your own.
Rule 5: If you ask a question, you deserve an answer.
Rule 6: Do not manipulate the buyer into giving you his or her name and telephone number.
Rule 7: Buyers don't call you back.
Rule 8: Buyers don't know what they want to buy.
Rule 9: Buyers have circled other ads besides yours.
Rule 10: Buyers who call on ads with a price usually can afford more.
Corollary: Buyers who call on signs usually can afford less.

Bonus Rule 1: Close early and often.
Bonus Rule 2: Always ask if the buyer has a house to sell. If so and he or she is in the area, you no longer have a buyer, you have a seller. If the buyer has a house to sell outside the area, you can send an outbound referral and make some additional money.

With buyers on the telephone, it is never too early to close, and you should close at every opportunity.

Generic Dialogue

Buyer: I am calling about a house I saw in the newspaper.

Salesperson: Great! Are you working with any other brokers to find you a house?

Buyer: Not at this time.

Salesperson: Are you looking for something kinda special?

Buyer: I'd like to think so.

Salesperson: I have a Preferred Clients group that sounds like it would be perfect for you. Let me tell you of its advantages.

This script will work with almost every buyer who calls. Later on in this chapter, we will address the specifics of this dialogue. But for now, learn the basics of this dialogue, and it will get you many more appointments than you are getting now. You may need to answer some more of the buyer's direct questions, but always work to get these dialogues into the conversation.

Additional Questions and Dialogue

If the buyer asks more questions, you as the salesperson can use the following questions to extend the conversation until you can work the generic dialogue into the conversation:

- Did you see our sign on that property?
- In which publication (or Web page) did you see the ad?
- Is that a neighborhood you are interested in?
- What is your time frame for moving?
- What amount of monthly payment will you be comfortable with?
- How much money do you have to invest in a home right now?
- Do you currently own your home, or do you rent?
- Do you have to sell before you buy?
- How much time is left on your lease, or are you month to month?
- When would be a good time for you and your spouse to meet with me?
- Are there any special features that you will require in your home?
- Have you purchased or sold property in this state in the last five years?
- Does your employer match in a 401(k) fund?
- How long do you plan on owning the home?
- Are you a veteran or married to one?
- Do you have an insurance policy that you can withdraw funds from for your down payment?
- Is your employer paying any of your closing costs?

- Tell me, what was it that caused you to call about that particular home?
- Was there anything else that particularly caught your eye?
- Wouldn't it be to your advantage to see more than one home in order to make the best possible selection for your future home?
- How long have you been looking for a home?
- It has three bedrooms. How many bedrooms do you need?
- What style of home do you prefer most?
- You know, Mr. Henderson, we have been told it is a bad real estate market, but in reality good properties sell very fast. Let me share with you how I work. I look at dozens of homes each week and have access to new properties the very moment they go on the market. What does this mean to you? It means that when I know what it is you like and—more important, what it is you don't like—when a property becomes available that meets your criteria, you will know about it before everyone else. What you see in the newspaper, on the Internet, or while driving by is rarely current or the best buy. You're getting only the tip of the iceberg of available properties. If you limit yourself to looking as you are currently doing, you are missing out on the only reliable resource for accurate, up-to-date properties—and that's me, your real estate professional. Then it's up to you whether you are interested in seeing the property or not. Does that make sense?
- Mr. Henderson, I know that sometimes it's difficult to commit to a single person or company, especially when you believe that you could find a home without that commitment. So if you would, allow me to tell you a little about

how I work and how my services will benefit you. My first and only responsibility is to those people who allow me the right of representing them in the purchase of a home. You can trust that my experience and knowledge will preserve your rights and that I will put you into the capable hands of experts in related services, such as loan origination, house inspections, title insurance—everything else you will need. If you ever have any questions, you will feel comfortable that the answers I give you are correct and true. If you are ready to begin the process, working with one professional is of great value to you. Can you see the benefits in that?

"Place on Hold" Dialogue

Salesperson: Hello. This is Dan Hamilton with Acme Realty.
How can I help you?
Buyer: I'm calling about the home on Colleen Court.
Salesperson: That is a very interesting home. Did you happen
to drive by the property?
Buyer: Yes.
Salesperson: Let me make sure it's still available and get the
file. Would you hold for just a moment, please?
Buyer: Yes.

The *Place on Hold Dialogue* is designed to give you a minute to not only get the property file but also gather your thoughts and adjust your attitude correctly.

The second statement by the salesperson is a generic response to make the buyer feel that he or she has chosen an interesting home. However, is it interesting in a good way or a bad way? The salesperson really does not need to take a position on that question, because it is all up to the buyer.

The salesperson then follows up that statement with a clarifying question: "Did you happen to drive by the property?" This question gives the salesperson a great deal of information. If the buyer has driven by the property, the salesperson will now know three things:

- The buyer probably likes the area. If not, he or she would not be interested in the property enough to call.
- The buyer is more likely to buy this house than if he or she were calling on an advertisement. Again, this is because he or she must like the neighborhood. (Still,

do not try to sell this property! Yes, the chances of selling are better, 8 percent, than they would be with an advertisement, 2 percent—but that percentage means that 92 percent of the time the buyer will buy something else.)

- The buyer probably cannot afford the house. Studies have shown that a typical buyer calling after driving by a property can afford less, maybe significantly less, than that property. (The buyer thinks, "If I could have this wonderful house in this wonderful neighborhood for $80,000, life would be wonderful!" Full of excitement, he or she calls the real estate company—and learns that the property is on the market for $280,000. This is why the professional real estate salesperson avoids revealing the price of the property before exploring other options with this potential buyer.)

The buyer may answer the salesperson's questions with "No, I am calling about an advertisement" (print, Web, or other). Studies have shown that a typical buyer can afford more, maybe significantly more, than the house he or she is calling about if he or she has seen the property in an advertisement with the price indicated. The buyer thinks, "If I could get everything I want in a home for $80,000, I would buy it in a second." Of course the $80,000 house is located in an area that this buyer will not like, or the property lacks the amenities that this buyer requires. Don't forget, though: this buyer has the means to pay much more to get what he or she wants.

The salesperson grabs the information on the property in question and any properties that are similar to it and gets back to the buyer quickly.

"Get the Name" Dialogue

Salesperson: Thank you for waiting. My name is Dan
   Hamilton. With whom am I speaking, please?
Buyer: Bob Henderson.
Salesperson: Thank you, Mr. Henderson.

You can probably get away with asking for the caller's name
at this time, but do not push it. The buyer may not feel that
you have earned the right to have his or her name this early,
so if you feel resistance, do not press the issue. Also, don't
ask for a telephone number, because that is overwhelming
to a buyer who does not like you or trust you yet.

   I have heard other trainers teach that if a buyer does not
give you his or her name, the agent should say, "Well, then
I will just call you Jack. Is that OK?" I hope those trainers are
kidding, because in real life that would get you slammed.

   Our objective for this call is to get an appointment.
Then, if we get an appointment, we have earned the right to
get the caller's name and telephone number.

"Provide Information" Dialogues

DIALOGUE I

Salesperson: I have the property file in front of me. Would you like for me to give you some information about this home?

Buyer: Sure.

Salesperson: That home has four bedrooms and two bathrooms with a custom kitchen and a wood fence around the backyard. The price of that home is $265,000. Is that more, less, or about the price range you were interested in?

Buyer: It is in our price range.

Salesperson: Fine. I could show that home to you at four o'clock or six o'clock. Which is better for you?

Notice that in the first dialogue line the salesperson uses the word "home" to refer to the property in question. This is because "home" is an extremely personal word and we want the buyer to relate to this property as his or her new home. The opposite is true with a seller: the salesperson would use the word "house" to distance the seller from the personal side of moving out of his or her home. This point may seem minor, but remember: *WORDS MEAN THINGS.*

The good thing about this dialogue is that as soon as the buyer said that this property was in his family's price range, the salesperson closed on an appointment. It may be too early to do so; the buyer will let you know that by asking more informational questions. But it can never hurt to attempt a close.

> **DIALOGUE II**
>
> The buyer could answer that the price is not right. Then use this dialogue:
>
> **Buyer:** Well, that's a little more than we would like to spend.
> **Salesperson:** Fine. What price range were you interested in?
> **Buyer:** No more than $200,000.
> **Salesperson:** I can arrange to show you some homes in that price range. When would it be convenient for you to see them? Today? Or would this weekend be better?

Most real estate salespeople think they are doing the buyers a service by giving them information and answering their questions. This helps no one except your competitors.

The buyers are seeking help, but if you let them, they will eliminate you. You must ask yourself, "Who is the best real estate salesperson for this buyer?" And your answer had better be "Me!" If not, you might want to look for another career.

Make no mistake about it. In the real estate business, we do not sell houses—we sell ourselves. Houses sell houses. If the buyers walk into the perfect house, they will buy it. We must get them to buy it from us to make any money, so in essence we are selling ourselves, not houses. And how can you sell something if you do not believe it is the best?

Most buyers who call are looking for information, but we are smart enough now to understand if we give a buyer too much information, he or she can eliminate that property and consequently eliminate us. Give just enough information—and then ask a quick question: "Is that more, less, or about the price range you were interested in?" This question is good, but somewhat dangerous. Remember: the buyer's objective is to eliminate that property, so if that property is not in his or her price range, the buyer can now eliminate it and us. We should use the following better and more powerful dialogue.

DIALOGUE III

Salesperson: I have the property file in front of me. Would you like for me to give you some information about that home?

Buyer: Sure.

Salesperson: That home has four bedrooms and two bathrooms with a custom kitchen and a wood fence around the backyard. The price of that home is $265,000. Are you working with any other real estate agents to find you a home?

Buyer: Uh, no, not at this time.

This dialogue is designed to move the buyer away from the property he or she called about as quickly as possible. As soon as the salesperson has discussed minor details of the home, he or she asks if the buyer is working with any other agents. Once the buyer answers no, the salesperson has control of the call, because he or she is asking the questions.

Suppose you use the *Provide Information Dialogue II* and the buyer can afford only $80,000 but the property costs $200,000. Can the buyer buy the $200,000 property? No. Can the buyer buy an $80,000 property? Yes. Is the buyer embarrassed enough that he or she no longer likes you? Probably. With the *Provide Information Dialogue III*, you no longer embarrass the buyer and can control that call and secure an appointment.

"Something Kinda Special" Dialogue

After moving the buyer away from the property that prompted the call, the salesperson should use the *Something Kinda Special Dialogue.*

Salesperson: From what you have said so far, let me ask you, are you looking for something kinda special?

Buyer: Of course.

Again, this dialogue is to drive the buyer further from the home he or she called about and to keep control of the conversation. The question is quite simple. I have never had a buyer say, "No, we are looking for a home that is a dump." Because there is only one way to answer this question, you have control of the next question.

"Doing Things the Hard Way" Dialogues

Now the buyer is set up for the *Doing Things the Hard Way Dialogue*.

DIALOGUE I

Salesperson: Mr. Henderson, you may be doing things the hard way. Do you know what I mean?

Buyer: No, not really.

Salesperson: Well, by driving around (or looking through the paper or checking the Web), you will find only a small percentage of the properties available at any one time. Not only that, but you will never find the really good values. Do you know why?

Buyer: I am not sure.

Salesperson: It is because you do not have access to the vast assortment of properties that I do. And the really good values go to what I call "Preferred Clients." To become Preferred Clients, buyers must come into our office and sit down with me so we can discuss the aspects of what they want in their next home. Then I can search the market of available properties and select some to show them. If nothing is to their liking, I continue my search. If a property of special interest comes onto the market, those Preferred Clients will be the first to know. Doesn't it make sense to become a Preferred Client if you are serious about finding the best home at the best price?

This *Doing Things the Hard Way Dialogue* allows the salesperson to show the buyer value in coming into the office. Buyers believe that they should call a real estate office and ask for a showing; then, if they like the property, they will buy it, and if not, they will call another real estate company for another showing. That's the same way as they went looking for an apartment. But hunting for a house is different. It's best to use one real estate salesperson—and that salesperson had better be you. You can only convert the buyers by showing value. As noted earlier in the chpater, this is the value for the buyer:

- Savings of money: By providing properties as they come onto the market, you will give the buyer the best chance at the best values.
- Savings of time: By having access to virtually all properties available for purchase on the Multiple Listing Service, you will reduce the amount of time spent driving around.
- Convenience of working with you: Once you know what the buyer wants, you can continue to search and preview properties for the buyer.

By offering to add the buyer to the Preferred Clients group (or whatever you choose to call it), you have created a special interest for the buyer. The only way the buyer can join this exclusive and valuable club is to come to the office and meet with you.

Also, notice that this dialogue uses lots of questions, as all dialogues should. Questions keep you in control and keep the buyer actively involved in the conversation.

DIALOGUE II

If you did not like the first dialogue, how do you feel about this one?

Salesperson: I tell you, you may be doing things the hard way. Let me tell you what I mean. You see, at any specific time a buyer will be exposed to only 5 or 10 percent of the market. Not all homes are advertised at one time. You will not drive past every home that would fit your desires. Even the Internet cannot make available all the properties that are on the market today. There is only one way to get the most properties to look at, and that is with me, your real estate professional. I have what I consider my Preferred Clients list. The only way to get onto that list is to come into the office and spend a few minutes with me and tell me about what you want in a home. From then on I can search all my vast sources and discover the right property before it reaches the mainstream. Most real values never last long on the market. Now, doesn't it make sense to become a Preferred Client?

DIALOGUE III

Here's one more for you!

Salesperson: I tell you, you may be doing things the hard way. Reports say that when people randomly look at properties like you want to do, they find one that actually interests them enough to buy it less than 2 percent of the time. Most buyers let the best properties slip away while they're looking at properties they will never like. Let me tell you what I mean. At any specific time a buyer will be exposed to only 5 or 10 percent of the market. Not all homes are advertised at one time. You will not drive past every home that would fit your desires. Even the Internet can't make available all the properties that are on the market today.

There is only one way to know about the most properties—and that's with me, your real estate professional. I have what I consider my Preferred Clients list. The only way to get onto that list is to come into the office and spend a few minutes telling me what you want in a home. From then on I can search all my vast sources and discover the right property before it reaches the mainstream. Most real values never last long on the market. Many buyers go out and look at property after property, and they never really see the best properties available. So if you look at that property, you are probably wasting your time because chances are you won't like it. Now, doesn't it make sense to become a Preferred Client?

DIALOGUE IV

This one is a little different, but aimed at the same target.

Salesperson: You know, sometimes the best homes are sold the day they come onto the market. I'd be happy to check our computer every morning for homes that might meet your needs, and I would let you know whenever I see anything new that could interest you. That way you'll have the most up-to-date information and the greatest chance of getting the home you want. Does that make sense to you?

Buyer: Yes, it does.

Salesperson: Great! Now, it will be very helpful for me to get a feel for exactly what you are looking for so that I don't waste your time with a lot of properties that don't fit your needs. How's today looking for you and your spouse to stop by and talk with me about your next home?

"Alternate Choice" Dialogue

Now that you have shown the buyer value in your services, it's time to close.

Salesperson: I am available now. Or would two o'clock be better for you to come into the office?

Buyer: Two o'clock would be great.

The *Alternate Choice Dialogue* is the most appropriate dialogue to close for an appointment. The alternate choice allows the buyer to choose between two times but does not allow him or her to say no. Anytime you want to make an appointment, use the *Alternate Choice Dialogue*.

"Wrap-Up" Dialogue

The *Wrap-Up Dialogue* is used to clean up any last-minute details before the phone conversation ends.

Buyer: We could see it at two o'clock.

Salesperson: Fine. Will there be someone else with you?

Buyer: My wife.

Salesperson: Great, if you have a pen handy, I'll give you our office address. OK?

Buyer: I have a pen.

Salesperson: The office is located at 1515 West Fifteenth Street. Are you familiar with that area?

Buyer: I can find it on my GPS.

Salesperson: All right. Again, my name is Dan Hamilton, and I look forward to meeting you at two o'clock. By the way, if your situation changes and you cannot keep this appointment, you will give me a call, won't you?

Buyer: Sure.

Salesperson: My cell number is 972-555-6789.

Buyer: Got it.

Salesperson: Good. I don't anticipate any problems from my end. But just in case, can I get your cell phone number?

Buyer: It's 817-555-1212.

Salesperson: Thanks. One last question. Are there any other properties that you've driven by that I could help you with?

Buyer: Well, we have a couple of others, but they're not with your company.

Salesperson: I can help you with those too, if you give me those addresses.

Buyer: That would be great. The first is at 1234 Elm, the second is at 4321 Smith, and the last one is at 15 Parkside Lane.

Salesperson: I will look those up also and have information on them when you and your wife get here at two o'clock. Any other questions?

Buyer: Not at this time.

Salesperson: See you at two. Bye now.

Buyer: Bye.

In the first part of this dialogue, you ask the buyer to identify who the "We" includes. It is critically important to determine who the decision makers are. Failure to determine this means that you and the buyers are wasting time.

In the second part, you ask if the buyer has a pen handy. This alerts the buyer that there is important information to follow and he or she should take notes.

Then you give the address of your office and make sure the buyer knows how to get there.

Next, you confirm the appointment time and give your phone number. This allows you to ask for the buyer's number.

Then you should ask if there are any other properties that the buyer has seen that are of interest, and you should offer to help. You must always ask this question each and every time prior to hanging up with a buyer.

We real estate salespeople get egotistical in believing when buyers call us that we have the only properties that are of interest to them. Not true! As a matter of fact, the buyers have usually circled several properties in the advertisement they are calling us about. Buyers believe that they must talk with the listing agent to see a property. We must educate them that we can help on any property. I have taken buyers from other real estate salespeople just because they did not ask this question. Don't let that happen to you!

"Get a Referral" Dialogues

These dialogues are designed to get you additional outbound referrals if you use them regularly with buyers who are selling their homes.

DIALOGUE I

Salesperson: Have you listed your home yet?
Buyer: Not yet.
Salesperson: I'd be happy to arrange a market evaluation for you with a local real estate company in Topeka. There's no obligation. But I will help you to know up front what kind of dollars you'll have to work with. That way, you can make an informed decision about whether you really want to buy in Maple Hills or in Happy Acres.

One of the most overlooked ways to make money in the real estate business is to get outbound referrals. Anytime you have a buyer on the telephone, you should find out if he or she has a house that must be sold before making the move to buy. If it is out of your area, you can send an outbound referral and make money when it sells.

DIALOGUE II

Salesperson: The Bob Smith Realty office will brief you on the real estate market in Topeka and give you a good idea of how long it will take to sell your place, when and if you make the big move.

"Lease-to-Buy Conversion" Dialogues

DIALOGUE I

Occasionally, a real estate sales office may get a call for a rental. Do not turn these potential buyers away. So many buyers think they can't buy when in reality they can. With a few of the right questions from these dialogues, you will be on your way to converting renters into buyers.

Buyer: I'm calling to see if you have any homes for rent.

Salesperson: If I could show you how to own your own home for less money each month than paying rent, would you consider buying a home at this time?

Buyer: Well, sure!

Salesperson: Fine. If you can spare a few minutes, I'd be happy to explain my program a little. May I set up a time that's convenient for you to come into the office and talk with me?

The first question is a great question to ask all renters. It could change your career!

DIALOGUE II

This dialogue is quite a bit longer and includes qualifying questions that are usually better to ask in person. But it will help the caller like and trust you if you ask them on the telephone.

Buyer: I'm calling to see if you have any homes for rent.

Salesperson: Can I ask you something first?

Buyer: Yes.

Salesperson: I am just curious because you asked me about renting, and over the years I have found that a lot of people who ask about renting would like to buy their own home. Most renters incorrectly believe it is impossible for them to be homeowners. Would you like to buy a home?"

Buyer: Yes, but I don't think I would qualify.

Salesperson: There are many, many great financial programs available now. Many are designed to help renters become homebuyers. Most of these programs offer very low initial investments and excellent terms. And if you cannot buy at this time, I have a system that will help you clean some stuff up and be able to buy in a short time. Also, I can tell you whether or not buying a home is an option at this time. Would you care to know if homeownership is a possibility for you?"

Buyer: Yes.

Salesperson: If you don't mind, we can do the preliminary questions right now. These questions may seem personal, but they must be answered to know if buying a home is an option. Is that OK with you?

Buyer: Sure.

Salesperson: Have you ever owned a home before?"

Buyer: No.

Salesperson: Approximately how much money could you come up with from any source—bank, family, and/or friends?

Buyer: Maybe $5,000. I could get a little more if I had to.

Salesperson: What is your approximate gross monthly income?

Buyer: $4,800.

Salesperson: Do you have many long-term monthly obligations?

Buyer: Well, I pay $400 per month for a truck.

Salesperson: How much are you paying in rent now?

Buyer: $850.

Salesperson: Do you have clean credit and a stable employment history?

Buyer: Yeah, I think so.

Salesperson: It looks like buying a home is an option for you. Let's schedule a time to complete the qualification process and discuss your home needs. I am available this afternoon. Which would be better for you, two o'clock or four o'clock?

Though this dialogue is much longer, it is more thorough. Sometimes potential buyers need convincing, and this dialogue is designed to do that.

BUYER QUESTIONS

Sometimes the buyer interrupts the flow of the above dialogue by asking questions. You must answer those questions, and then follow up by asking a question of your own. Always look to show value and close.

"Owner Finance" Dialogues

DIALOGUE I

Buyer: Will the owner finance the down payment?

Salesperson: I really couldn't make that decision for the owner, and the data sheet does not indicate that the owner would. Is owner financing important to you?"

Buyer: Yes.

Salesperson: The owner seems to be flexible. But of course I can't guarantee it. When would you like to see the home? At two o'clock? Or would four be better?

Buyer: We could see it at four o'clock.

The salesperson handled the question and then asked a question. Once the buyer answered, the salesperson used the *Alternate Choice Dialogue.*

DIALOGUE II

Buyer: Will the owner finance the down payment?

Salesperson: I really couldn't make that decision for the owner and the data sheet does not indicate that the owner would. Have you spoken to a lender to see if you could qualify?

Buyer: No.

Salesperson: Fine. Are you looking for something kinda special?

Buyer: Well, sure.

This dialogue shifts the buyer away from the house by asking about his or her loan situation. Then the salesperson goes to the *Something Kinda Special Dialogue.*

"Meet at Property" Dialogue

Buyer: Can't we just meet at the house?

Salesperson: The problem is that we cannot take care of the things necessary to put you on the Preferred Clients list. And I am sure you understand the value of having someone like me work for you, don't you?

Buyer: Well, yes.

Salesperson: Great! Now I am available at two o'clock. Or would four be better?

With this dialogue the salesperson hardly acknowledges the question, handling it by offering the value located in the *Doing Things the Hard Way Dialogue*. Here again, the salesperson uses the *Alternate Choice Dialogue* to close for the appointment. Sometimes you have already addressed the buyer's question, so it may be best just to assume that he or she wants to come into the office. That is how this dialogue and the next one work.

"I Am Not Paying" Dialogue

Occasionally the buyers think that what you are offering is too good to be true, so they believe they will have to pay to be on the Preferred Clients list. You never want to say it is free, because then it does not seem of value. Let's see how to handle this.

Buyer: Well, I am not paying you anything.

Salesperson: Would you want to have all the services I can offer and not pay for them?

Buyer: How can you do that?

Salesperson: Meet me at the office at two o'clock, and we will discuss how that is possible. Fair enough?

With this dialogue, you again are assuming that the buyer will come in at two o'clock, and you ask a question to set that up. Never discuss the payment of your fee over the telephone—you will always lose!

"Drive By and Call You" Dialogues

DIALOGUE I

Some buyers don't want to meet you, so their way out is to tell you that they will drive by and call you. Always remember: the biggest lie in real estate is "I will call you."

Buyer: Just give me the address, and we'll ride by and take a look, and if it is something that we like, we will call you.

Salesperson: I'd be happy to do that. However, the seller has requested I accompany all showings. When were you planning on riding by?

Buyer: At about two o'clock.

Salesperson: Fine. I am available at that time. Would you prefer to meet me at my office, or shall I pick you up?

This dialogue is easy, but not as effective as it could be. Some buyers are willing to meet with you with very little convincing. Others may be more difficult. However, you should be able to convert either type into an appointment.

DIALOGUE II

Buyer: I don't want to waste your time. We can just drive by if you will give me the exact address.

Salesperson: I really would like to do that, but the seller wants me to accompany all showings. Let me ask you this: if I were representing you, would you want me to just arbitrarily give out information about your home?

Buyer: I guess not.

Salesperson: I promise not to inconvenience you in any way as I show you the home. It will only take a few minutes to show it to you, and I'll stay out of your way. Fair enough?

Chapter 2
Telemarketing for Real Estate
Agents and Brokers

The real estate industry has never been much on prospecting for clients to buy or sell real estate. All real estate professionals know and understand the benefits of prospecting, but few actually have a program to continually prospect for clients. This chapter is intended to provide real estate practitioners dialogues that will give them the knowledge and confidence to make telephone calls.

This chapter presents and discusses the following:

- A list of assumptions for telemarketing
- Dialogues on generic telemarketing
- Dialogues for doing surveys
- Dialogues on telemarketing about a specific property
- Dialogues on telemarketing for a specific person
- Dialogues for specific situations
- Dialogues for communicating with people in your sphere of influence

This chapter is intended for the sales professional who understands the value of prospecting for business. It is specifically designed to benefit the salesperson by providing the dialogues necessary to call on prospects. These prospects turn into clients, and those clients turn into dollars. Without the information given in this chapter, the salesperson would be left to design relevant dialogues the hard way, by trial and error.

These are the objectives of this chapter:

- Be able to list the assumptions for telemarketing.
- Be able to use effectively the dialogues given throughout the chapter.
- Be able to recite the benefits of each of the dialogues for earning commission dollars.
- Be able to differentiate among the dialogues and determine which one should be used in any particular situation.

Telemarketing—aka Cold Calling

Telemarketing is calling people to find out if they are thinking about buying or selling real estate. It is also called cold calling, warm calling, telephone prospecting, and gold calling. I don't care what you call it. Just get on the phone!

Here we will mainly concentrate on calling owners of real estate, because they are the easiest to control and the best for building a successful real estate career. Buyers of real estate are great, but harder to control and more difficult to prospect. If you get the listings, you will get the buyers.

The following are a few of the assumptions that need to be made when telemarketing:

- **Assumption 1:** When you ask the question, the prospect will always be set back a little.
- **Assumption 2:** The longer you can keep the prospect on the telephone, the better.

- **Assumption 3:** It is crucial to create motivation.
- **Assumption 4:** The number you are calling is scrubbed against the National Do Not Call Registry and is not on the registry.

Generic Telemarketing Dialogues

GENERIC DIALOGUE I

Salesperson: Hello, is this Mr. Vinson?

Homeowner: Yes.

Salesperson: My name is Dan Hamilton with Acme Realty. Have you thought about selling your house now or in the near future?

Homeowner: No.

Salesperson: Thanks. Bye.

Let's review the advantages of this dialogue. Anyone can use the *Generic Telemarketing Dialogue*. You can call any neighborhood at any time.

Here are a couple of quick thoughts. First, notice how fast you get to your main question—the first question. This is important because people don't want to talk with you any more than you want to talk with telemarketers. Get to the question and get off the telephone. If you don't waste their time, people don't get angry. Also, the sooner you get off the telephone with someone who is not interested, the sooner you can find someone who is interested. If you get an answering machine, leave a message, using the same dialogue. Be sure to leave a telephone number so the prospect can return your call.

GENERIC DIALOGUE II

Salesperson: Hello, is this Mr. Vinson?

Homeowner: Who's calling?

Salesperson: My name is Dan Hamilton with Acme Realty. Have you thought about selling your house now or in the near future?

> ***Homeowner:*** Yes.
>
> ***Salesperson:*** Do you have a second to tell me a little about your house?

The difference is that this time the homeowner said yes. The follow-up question, "Do you have a second to tell me a little about your house?" is a great question for many reasons. When you call homeowners who are not expecting your call and ask if they have ever thought of selling their home, they may be a little skeptical of your motives. Also, you may be a little nervous talking with a live prospect. This question helps relieve any tension for the homeowner because he or she knows the house and can relax and tell you about it in detail. While the homeowner talks, you have time to settle your nerves and get the listing appointment. Besides, you need that information from the homeowner for your property analysis and for pricing the property correctly. To get all the information you need, you should post a list of questions by your telephone.

The homeowner asked the question, "Who's calling?" This indicates you have reached the right person, but he or she does not know you. You should continue with the dialogue as written. If the person is interested, he or she will tell you. If not, then end the call.

Be consistent in your telemarketing. You may not get a listing out of your first call, but eventually you will succeed.

GENERIC DIALOGUE III

> ***Salesperson:*** Hi, this is Dan Hamilton with Acme Realty, and I was wondering, are you considering selling your home now or in the near future?

Homeowner: Yes, we're thinking about it.

Salesperson: When would that be?

Homeowner: Right away.

Salesperson: When would be a good time for us to meet so I may show you how I can get your home sold in the least amount of time and for the most money? Would this evening be good for you, or would tomorrow evening be better?

This dialogue is easy, but not as effective in putting the homeowner at ease. The homeowner is very interested, so closing early is appropriate. The salesperson used the *Alternate Choice Dialogue* to close for the appointment, as presented in Chapter 1.

GENERIC DIALOGUE IV

Salesperson: Hi, this is Dan Hamilton with Acme Realty, and I was wondering, are you considering selling your home now or in the near future?

Homeowner: Yes, we've thought about it, but not now, maybe in about a year.

Salesperson: As a professional real estate agent, I see property every day and know what it takes to market your home so you can get the best price in the shortest amount of time with the least inconvenience to you. I would be more than happy to share with you some preliminary marketing ideas, so when you're ready to put your home on the market, we will be prepared to get it sold. When would be a good time for us to meet? Would this evening be good for you, or would tomorrow evening be better?

This dialogue is intended to get the salesperson into the house now. Waiting is never best. The sooner you can get into the house, the sooner you can make a good impression on the homeowner. Then you must follow up regularly to ensure that the homeowner will list with you when the time arrives.

GENERIC DIALOGUE V

Salesperson: Hi, this is Dan Hamilton with Acme Realty, and I was wondering, are you considering selling your home now or in the near future?

Homeowner: Yes, we've thought about it, but it won't be for several years.

Salesperson: May I put your name and address into my database so that I can keep you informed about market conditions? It will also give you the opportunity to contact me at any time in the future should you have any real estate questions or needs.

Again, this is follow-up. Several years in real estate can pass quickly, so it almost seems like yesterday. Fill up your database with these people. I can tell you they will do what they say: when that time arrives, you will be the one they will call.

Calling to Do Survey

SURVEY DIALOGUE I

Salesperson: Hi! This is Dan Hamilton with Acme Realty. We're doing a quick telephone survey in the area. May I ask you a few questions?

Homeowner: I guess.

Salesperson: When do you plan on moving?

Homeowner: I don't know. It will be a while.

Salesperson: How long have you lived at this address?

Homeowner: Eight years.

Salesperson: Where did you move from?

Homeowner: We moved from El Paso, Texas.

Salesperson: How did you happen to pick this area?

Homeowner: We liked the trees and the quiet feel.

Salesperson: If you were to move, where would you go?

Homeowner: We would really like to go to the lake.

Salesperson: When would that be?

Homeowner: Well, I would like to move as soon as possible, but I don't know if we can get the money that we need out of this house.

Salesperson: When would be a good time for the two of you and me to get together so I can show you how I can help you sell your home in the shortest amount of time and for the most money? If we can't get the money out of it, then we haven't lost a thing. Would this evening be good for you, or would tomorrow evening be better?

With this dialogue the salesperson is asking a lot of questions for a survey. Once complete, the survey will add valuable data for you to use in marketing to this area. The down-side to the survey is in the first line, because we have to ask permission. The homeowner can tell us no before we can even ask if he or she has thought about selling. In the end the homeowner admitted to thinking about moving, but felt that it might not be possible to get the money out of the property. This shift will happen because we spend some time asking questions. The questions are not as important as showing that we care about the homeowner's situation.

SURVEY DIALOGUE II

Salesperson: Hi! This is Dan Hamilton with Acme Realty. We're doing a quick telephone survey in the area. May I ask you a few questions?

Homeowner: I guess.

Salesperson: When do you plan on moving?

Homeowner: I don't know. It will be a while.

Salesperson: How long have you lived at this address?

Homeowner: Eight years.

Salesperson: Where did you move from?

Homeowner: We moved from El Paso, Texas.

Salesperson: How did you happen to pick this area?

Homeowner: We liked the trees and the quiet feel.

Salesperson: If you were to move, where would you go?

Homeowner: We would really like to go to the lake.

Salesperson: When would that be?

Homeowner: Probably three to five years, when my husband retires.

Salesperson: As a professional real estate agent, I see homes every day and know what it takes to market your home so you can get the best price in the shortest amount of time with the least inconvenience to you. I would be more than happy to share with you some pre-marketing ideas, so that when you're ready to put your home on the market we will be prepared to get it sold. When would be a good time for you and your husband to meet with me? Would this evening be good for you, or would tomorrow evening be better?

In this dialogue the wife says that she and her husband will move when he retires in three to five years. Again, this is a short amount of time, so the salesperson attempts to close her for an appointment at this time. If she says no, the salesperson should offer to bring the results of the survey.

If the time is longer than five years to move, the salesperson should use the following dialogue.

SURVEY DIALOGUE III

Salesperson: May I put your name into my database so that I can keep you informed about market conditions? It will also give you the opportunity to call me at any time in the future should you have real estate questions or needs.

Even though these homeowners are a long time from selling, the salesperson should follow up on them. Having a database full of future sellers is incredibly valuable for your future income. The follow-up does not have to be intense. A postcard every month offering something of value would do the trick. Follow-up should not be a burden to the salesperson.

Calling about a Specific Property

SPECIFIC PROPERTY DIALOGUE I

Salesperson: Hello, is this Mrs. Vinson?

Homeowner: Yes.

Salesperson: My name is Dan Hamilton with Acme Realty. I am calling to see if you have considered selling your house either now or in the near future. Have you?

Homeowner: No.

Salesperson: The reason I ask is that we recently listed (sold) a house near yours on Colleen Court, and as a result of our extensive advertising, we have generated quite a bit of interest for homes in this area and we need more properties. Do you know anyone thinking about selling? How about you?

Homeowner: Yes.

Salesperson: Do you have a second to tell me a little about your house?

The reason the homeowner says yes the second time is because it now seems that you have an actual reason for calling. A random call is startling or suspicious unless the person receiving the call knows the reason. Needless to say, you must actually have sold a house on Colleen Court. Never lie to potential clients, or anyone for that matter.

Some real estate experts say it could be a listing by any company. In that case, you would change the dialogue just a bit: "The reason I ask is that a house near yours recently was listed/sold." Notice you don't use the word "we" when you use other companies' listings and sales. Please consult your broker and the rules of your association before using a *Specific Property Dialogue* based on a listing by another company.

One final thought: you would not use this dialogue if the homeowner's voice is harsh in the beginning. If you ask, "Have you ever thought about selling?" and the homeowner shouts, "No!" end the call. Use the *Specific Property Dialogue* if you hear some hesitation in the person's words—"Uh, well, no." He or she may be thinking about it but feel unsure about the situation. If you continue the conversation, it will give the homeowner a chance to calm down and say yes.

SPECIFIC PROPERTY DIALOGUE II

Salesperson: Mrs. Vinson?

Homeowner: Yes.

Salesperson: This is Dan Hamilton from Acme Realty. I thought you'd be interested in knowing that we sold the property on Colleen Court just down the street from you. In the process, we discovered a lot a people interested in the neighborhood. Do you know of anyone else who might be ready to sell in the near future?

Homeowner: No, I sure don't.

Salesperson: Have you thought about selling?

Homeowner: No, not at this time.

Salesperson: Well, thanks for taking the time to talk with me.

This call is a must. It proves to the homeowner that you actually sell property. When and if this homeowner decides to sell, you have an advantage over all other real estate salespeople. Not all sales calls have to result in a sale to be productive. This homeowner could have said yes, but did not. It still is an effective sales call for your future income.

SPECIFIC PROPERTY DIALOGUE III

Salesperson: Hello, Mrs. Henderson?

Homeowner: Yes.

Salesperson: My name is Dan Hamilton, and I'm with Acme Real Estate. Do you have a moment to talk?

Homeowner: What's this about?

Salesperson: I wanted to let you know that the house on Colleen Court has sold. I've been doing some research on your neighborhood. Would you be interested in knowing the average price of houses like yours? (Would you be interested in a free market evaluation of your house?)

Homeowner: Not at this time.

Salesperson: Have you thought about moving?

Homeowner: Sure. Hasn't everybody?

Salesperson: If you were to move, when would that be?

Homeowner: Not for a while.

Salesperson: Do you know anybody who might be interested in buying or selling a home? Are any of your relatives, friends, neighbors, or co-workers thinking about moving?

Homeowner: I don't think so.

Salesperson: Thank you for your time and help.

This dialogue shows how you can keep the potential client on the telephone as long as possible without becoming abusive. The longer the homeowner stays on the telephone, the more it indicates his or her interest in moving. The dialogue ends with a further question about other potential clients.

SPECIFIC PROPERTY DIALOGUE IV

Salesperson: My name is Dan Hamilton representing Acme

Realty. I'm sorry to bother you, but may I ask you a quick question?

Homeowner: Yes.

Salesperson: I have a very nice home for sale in your area at a very good price. Can you think of a friend or relative that you would like to have as a neighbor?

Homeowner: Yes, one of my friends has said she wants to live in the area.

Salesperson: May I give her a call to tell her about it and use your name?

This dialogue demonstrates what some trainers suggest, to open with an apology. I understand the purpose, but you should think this through. Are you offering a valuable service? The answer had better be a resounding "Yes!" or maybe real estate is not your career. If the answer is yes, then why are you apologizing? I suggest you do not need to apologize when your service is valuable. If you feel you need to apologize, this following is your dialogue.

SPECIFIC PROPERTY DIALOGUE V

Salesperson: I just got a new listing in the neighborhood. It's a great value. Would you know anyone who is interested in moving into this neighborhood?

This dialogue is a simple variation of the above dialogue IV.

SPECIFIC PROPERTY DIALOGUE VI

Salesperson: I've recently placed the Henderson house just down the street from you on the market for $245,000. I was wondering if you might be thinking about selling. Or maybe you know some friends moving to the area?

This dialogue is very specific about the property, making the call sound more legitimate. The negative side of this dialogue is that most homeowners want more for their property than it is worth. This dialogue could generate a dispute before we have time to build rapport.

SPECIFIC PROPERTY DIALOGUE VII

Salesperson: Hello, Mrs. Vinson?

Homeowner: Yes.

Salesperson: My name is Dan Hamilton with Acme Realty. My office has recently sold the property on Colleen Court. I thought you might like to know the selling price. I believe the value of that home will greatly affect the value of yours. May I tell you about it?

Homeowner: Yes, I guess.

Salesperson: The house has over 2,000 square feet with a double garage and features an open concept. The backyard is typical for the neighborhood. The property sold for $230,000. By the way, we find that when a home sells, the activity created by that sale attracts many additional buyers to the neighborhood. With that in mind, I was wondering if you have any interest in selling your home. How long have you owned your property?

Homeowner: 11 years.

Salesperson: Wow, that's a while. Have you ever thought about moving again?

Homeowner: Oh, occasionally.

Salesperson: Any particular time frame?

Homeowner: Probably after my husband retires, which isn't for another year.

Salesperson: Could I continue to stay in touch, providing you with relevant market information in your area?

This dialogue is very specific in describing the property, which allows the homeowner to picture the home and mentally compare it with his or hers. If the homeowner feels that his or her house is better, it could motivate a decision to sell.

SPECIFIC PROPERTY DIALOGUE VIII

Salesperson: Mrs. Vinson, this is Dan Hamilton again with Acme Realty. I thought you'd be interested in knowing that we did sell the Henderson property. In the process, we discovered a lot of people interested in the neighborhood. Do you know of anyone else who might be ready to sell in the near future?

Homeowner: No, we don't.

Salesperson: Have you changed your mind about selling?

Homeowner: No, we haven't.

This dialogue proves that you can sell real estate, not just market it. When homeowners believe property is moving, they begin thinking more seriously about selling—and sooner rather than later.

SPECIFIC PROPERTY DIALOGUE IX

Salesperson: Hi! This is Dan Hamilton with Acme Realty. I wanted to let you know that I just sold the home on the corner of Allen Avenue and Brittany Boulevard, and I'm wondering if you've considered selling your home either now or in the near future.

Homeowner: Well, we have talked about it.

Salesperson: Great! How soon would you want into your next place?

Homeowner: You know, the truth is that there is no way for at least two years.

Salesperson: As a real estate professional, I see homes every day and know what it takes to market your home so that you can get the best price in the shortest amount of time. I would be more than happy to share with you some ideas that you could begin doing now, so that when you're ready to put your house on the active market, we will be prepared to get it sold. I would be glad to share my thoughts with you. Now, I am available this evening. Or would tomorrow evening be better for us to meet?

This dialogue is a variation of the above dialogue, with a longer time frame before selling. Stay in touch with these homeowners regularly because their time frame could change for any number of reasons.

SPECIFIC PROPERTY DIALOGUE X

Salesperson: Hi! This is Dan Hamilton with Acme Realty. I wanted to let you know that I just sold the home on the corner of Allen Avenue and Brittany Boulevard, and I'm wondering if you've considered selling your home either now or in the near future.

Homeowner: Well, we have talked about it.

Salesperson: Great! How soon would you want to move into your next home?

Homeowner: Not until my son graduates from high school, and that won't be for three years.

Salesperson: May I continue to keep you informed on market changes so you will be informed and knowledgeable when your time comes to sell? It will also give you the opportunity to contact me at any time in the future should you have real estate questions or needs.

In this dialogue, the time to sell is even further away. This means more follow-up, but it's a great database contact.

SPECIFIC PROPERTY DIALOGUE XI

Salesperson: Hello, Mrs. Vinson?

Homeowner: Yes.

Salesperson: My name is Dan Hamilton with Acme Realty, and I just represented the Allens during their purchase of the home on Colleen Court. The Allens are from California, and I am sure they would appreciate it if, the next time you see them, you would welcome them into the area.

Homeowner: Sure, I could do that.

Salesperson: Great! By the way, when a home sells in a neighborhood, it usually stimulates a lot of buyer interest in the area. It would be a great time to market your home. Are you planning a move?

This dialogue appeals to the hospitality of the homeowner and then inquires about any interest in selling.

Calling Specific Person

SPECIFIC PERSON DIALOGUE I

Salesperson: Hello, this is Dan Hamilton with Acme Realty. The reason for my call is that I have been working with a buyer who wants to live in your neighborhood. I have already shown her all the houses on the market, and she hasn't found what she's looking for. I told her I would call around the neighborhood to see if I might find someone who is thinking about selling. Are you considering selling your home at this time?

Homeowner: No.

Salesperson: Thanks. Goodbye.

This dialogue is the best cold-call dialogue, because we have a specific person for whom we are calling to find a house. This opportunity may sound too good to be true to a homeowner, so be ready to give some nonconfidential details about your buyer. Again, you must have a buyer. But it's not hard to get a buyer on whose behalf you can call. Just ask your next buyer if you can call around a neighborhood for him or her. The buyer will think you are great, and you will have your reason to call.

SPECIFIC PERSON DIALOGUE II

Salesperson: Hello, this is Dan Hamilton with Acme Realty. The reason for my call is that I have been working with a buyer who wants to live in your neighborhood. I have already shown her all the houses on the market, and she hasn't found what she's looking for. I told her I would call around the neighborhood to see if I might find someone who is thinking about selling. Are you considering selling your home at this time?

Homeowner: Yes.

Salesperson: Do you have a second to tell me a little about your house?

Same dialogue as before, but the homeowner's answer is affirmative.

SPECIFIC PERSON DIALOGUE III

Salesperson: Hello, Mrs. Vinson?

Homeowner: Yes.

Salesperson: My name is Dan Hamilton with Acme Realty. Have you thought about selling your house?

Homeowner: No.

Salesperson: The reason I ask is that I'm working for a couple by the name of Henderson, and they're looking for a home in your area. We haven't found anything, and I promised I'd talk with homeowners in the area until I found the right house. Do you happen to know of anyone selling?

Homeowner: No, I don't know of anyone.

Salesperson: How about you?

This dialogue uses the buyer's name. The use of a name lends credibility to the dialogue. Be prepared to answer questions about your buyer. You could give the homeowner general information about your buyer but nothing nothing confidential.

SPECIFIC PERSON DIALOGUE IV

Salesperson: Hello, Mrs. Vinson?

Homeowner: Yes.

Salesperson: This is Dan Hamilton with Acme Realty. I was wondering if you could help me for a moment. I'm working with a family from California who are relocating to this area. We spent last weekend looking at neighborhoods and schools. Your property is in one of the three neighborhoods they're interested in. The problem is that there are very few houses on the market here right now that meet their needs. Have you have ever considered moving?

Homeowner: No, I haven't.

Salesperson: Have you heard that any of your neighbors might be planning to move?

Homeowner: No.

Salesperson: OK. I will drop you a business card in the mail today so that you can reach me if you hear of anyone wanting to move. Thanks now.

Homeowners believe that out-of-state buyers are much more serious. If your buyer is from out of state, use this dialogue.

SPECIFIC PERSON DIALOGUE V

Salesperson: The reason I ask is I'm working with a couple who have recently gotten jobs in the area and have children and love this part of town. Now they're looking for a home in your neighborhood. We haven't found them anything yet, and I promised them I'd talk with every homeowner in the area until I found the right house. Do you happen to know of anyone interested in selling?

This dialogue is similar to the previous ones, except now you mention that the family lives locally and has children.

You may want to get permission from your buyers to mention that they have children, but if they really want to live in that neighborhood, they will not mind. Mentioning that they have children makes the buyers more personable.

SPECIFIC PERSON DIALOGUE VI

Salesperson: I'm working with a couple who are interested in living in your neighborhood. Would you know any neighbors who might be interested in selling their home?

This is one more variation that indicates a couple, which further indicates stability.

Calling an Out-of-Town Agent

Use this dialogue to solicit the listing from an agent that has listed a property well outside his or her market area. Generally, agents do not want to work a listing at a distance, but do not know whom to refer it to.

Salesperson: Hi, Bob! My name is Dan Hamilton with Acme Realty here in Fort Worth. I've noticed that you have taken a listing on Colleen Court in our city. I've also noticed that your telephone number indicates you live quite some distance from the listed property. I'm hoping that I could help you avoid the hassles of a distance listing by offering to partner with you on this property. All you would have to do is introduce me to your clients and transfer the listing to me, and I will pay you a referral fee at closing. I have a great deal of experience selling properties like this one and would love the opportunity to help you and your client. Does this sound like a fair proposal?

Calling a Waif

CALLING A WAIF DIALOGUE I

A waif is a person who has had a relationship with a real estate salesperson and now has been abandoned. Many real estate salespeople do one or two transactions and then quit real estate, abandoning their clients. By contacting these clients, a real estate salesperson could add a multitude of new contacts to his or her database. These waifs probably had good experiences and would love to hear from a real estate professional on a regular basis.

Salesperson: Mr. Henderson?

Homeowner: Yes.

Salesperson: My name is Dan Hamilton, and I am one of the most respected real estate representatives for Acme Realty. I understand that Bob Johnson from Acme sold you this home?

Homeowner: Yes, he did.

Salesperson: He is no longer able to serve your needs, so I wanted to make sure you are taken care of. How do you like the home you purchased from us?

Homeowner: We like it just fine.

Salesperson: Well, that is good to hear. It is our objective to be sure your real estate needs are met. Is there any other real estate need that you have or any that someone you know has?

Homeowner: Not at this time.

Salesperson: Have you ever thought about investment property?

Homeowner: No, not really.

Salesperson: Well, OK! If there ever is anything I can do for you, remember: I am your resource for real estate information.

After this call, you will want to follow up monthly with market data or other relevant information. If the homeowner is not happy with the service provided by the previous salesperson, use the following dialogue.

CALLING A WAIF DIALOGUE II

Salesperson: Mr. Henderson?

Homeowner: Yes.

Salesperson: My name is Dan Hamilton, and I am one of the most respected real estate representatives for Acme Realty. I understand that Bob Johnson from Acme sold you this home?

Homeowner: Yes, he did.

Salesperson: He is no longer able to serve your needs, so I wanted to make sure you are taken care of. How do you like the home you purchased from us?

Homeowner: Actually, we are very upset.

Salesperson: Would you like to share with me your concerns?

Homeowner: Bob got several thousand dollars, and we feel we were left to fend for ourselves.

Salesperson: I am sorry to hear that. Is there anything I can do at this point?

Homeowner: It's too late now.

Salesperson: Could I keep you aware of market conditions in your area?

Homeowner: No chance! I have dealt with your company once already!

Salesperson: Mr. Henderson, if you had a salesperson who did not provide a customer the service that the customer deserves, what would you do with that salesperson?

Homeowner: I would fire him!

Salesperson: Exactly—and let someone take care of the customer who is qualified to provide valuable service. Is that correct?

Homeowner: I get it. You are that person, right?

Salesperson: Could I keep you aware of market conditions in your area?

Homeowner: Yes, please do.

Notice that I never said that the previous salesperson was fired, but I also want to ensure that I won't be the same. Time heals all wounds, and generally these calls go smoothly.

Calling on a Mail-Out Card

This dialogue would be used after you have sent a mail-out into an area. Studies have shown that a mail-out followed by a personal telephone call results in a higher rate of return.

Salesperson: Hello. My name is Dan Hamilton with Acme Realty. Last week I sent you an update on the real estate activity in your neighborhood. I was calling to see if I could answer any questions or you needed any more information?

Homeowner: No, I don't have any questions.

Salesperson: Have you ever thought about selling your home, either now or in the near future?

Homeowner: Not at this time.

Salesperson: Have you ever thought about real estate as a possible investment?

Homeowner: No, I haven't.

Salesperson: Thank you for your time, and I am here as your real estate resource.

This dialogue adds the idea about investments. Many homeowners are not interested in selling their homes, but are very interested in buying and selling real property or buying and renting real property. If you don't ask, you will never know.

Calling a For Rent By Owner

DIALOGUE I

A high percentage of landlords do not want to be landlords; they kind of fell into it. It took too long for them to sell a property, and they rented it simply to get some money coming in from the property. This dialogue is to stir up the interest to sell once again.

Salesperson: Hello, my name is Dan Hamilton with Acme Realty, and I'm calling about the property in the newspaper for rent. Would you consider selling it?

Homeowner: Yes, I would if I got my price.

Salesperson: Great! Would you mind if I stopped by and took a quick look at the place?

Short, sweet, and to the point—always the best type of dialogue.

DIALOGUE II

Salesperson: Hello, my name is Dan Hamilton with Acme Realty, and I'm calling about the property in the newspaper for rent. Would you consider selling it?

Homeowner: No, I don't want to sell.

Salesperson: I understand. If I found an investment-grade property in that area, would you like for me to give you a call?

This dialogue begins in the same way, but twists at the end. We now ask the landlord if he or she would like more property. Any true investor always is on the lookout for more property. Key words here are "investment grade." That term could mean almost anything, so now we can call this investor on any type of property.

Calling Someone with Positive Life Changes

One of the most frequent reasons to sell a property and buy another is a life change. The owners are adding a new baby. Their children have graduated. An owner has been elected city mayor. An owner has received a huge promotion (noted in the daily newspaper). This dialogue would be used.

Salesperson: Hello, Mr. Jones. My name is Dan Hamilton with Acme Realty. I wanted to call and congratulate you on your new promotion. I am sure you are excited. I was also wondering if you have reconsidered your current real estate needs.

Any such life change could result in a real estate need, and the first salesperson to call will get this transaction.

Calling Someone with Negative Life Changes

This dialogue is the same as the previous dialogue, except that the life change is negative. These calls can be tough: not all real estate professionals will want to talk with these homeowners. However, we offer a service that may well be needed at this time. Negative reasons could include empty nest syndrome (no more children living at home), health issues, and death of a family member.

Salesperson: Hello, Mr. Jones. My name is Dan Hamilton with Acme Realty. I wanted to call and offer my condolences to you and your family. If there is anything I can do during this time, please let me know.

The discussion from here would depend upon how the homeowner reacts. Sometimes it is best to just make contact and then wait for a while before contacting the person again.

Calling Someone Who Wants Your Phone Number

Occasionally, you will get the jokester that thinks it is funny to try and set you up. It is best to stay professional and not let the person get to you. Here is the most professional way to handle such a situation.

Salesperson: Hello, Mr. Vinson. This is Dan Hamilton from Acme Realty. I'm calling because....

Homeowner: I'm busy right now. Give me your home number, and I'll call you later.

Salesperson: Not a problem. My cell phone is 972-555-6789, and my office phone is 214-555-1755. If I miss your call, please leave a message, and I will call right back. If my message service says someone called and didn't leave a message, I'll assume it was you and call you right away. Thank you very much for your time. If you ever have a real estate need or question, please call. My name is Dan Hamilton from Acme Realty. Once again, thank you.

The latest one to make the rounds is for the homeowner to pretend to be a police officer at a crime scene. If this one happens to you, just turn it around and ask the officer for his or her name and badge number. Whatever you do, stay calm. The person is just trying to get you riled. Don't let the jokester succeed. You need to stay professional.

One last thing: don't automatically assume this is going to happen to you. It may never happen, but be prepared.

Calling about a Great Property

GREAT PROPERTY DIALOGUE I

Salesperson: Mrs. Vinson, this is Dan Hamilton from Acme Realty. I sent a letter to you two days ago, and I wanted to make sure you received it. Do you remember receiving a letter from me?

Homeowner: Yes.

Salesperson: I wrote to you because we have an incredible offering on a property on Colleen Court. It is a larger home than the one you live in now, a great investment rental property. It has four bedrooms and three bathrooms with a pool and other amenities. And it's priced to sell quickly. I wanted you to be one of the first to know about the property. Is this something in which you or someone you know might have an interest?

Homeowner: Yes, I might be interested.

Salesperson: Great! When can you come into the office and discuss the details and take a look at the property? I am available today. Or would tomorrow be better?

Everybody wants a great investment. Offering this to your potential clients may motivate them to actually make a commitment.

GREAT PROPERTY DIALOGUE II

Salesperson: Mrs. Vinson, this is Dan Hamilton from Acme Realty. I sent a letter to you two days ago, and I wanted to make sure you received it. Do you remember receiving a letter from me?

Homeowner: Yes.

Salesperson: I wrote to you because we have an incredible offering on a property on Colleen Court. It is a larger home than the one you live in now, a great investment rental property. It has four bedrooms and three bathrooms with a pool and other amenities. And it's priced to sell quickly. I wanted you to be one of the first to know about the property. Is it something in which you or someone you know might have an interest?

Homeowner: No, I wouldn't be interested.

Salesperson: I see you purchased your home in 2004. Is that when you moved into the area?

Homeowner: Yes, that is correct.

Salesperson: Are you still happy with your home?

Homeowner: Not particularly.

Salesperson: Are you planning to make a move in the future?

Homeowner: We will probably move once our youngest graduates. So I guess that would be in another two years.

Salesperson: Mrs. Vinson, thank you for your time. If you ever have a real estate need or question, please e-mail me. Again, my name is Dan Hamilton from Acme Realty. My e-mail address is simply my name, Dan Hamilton, at Acme Realty dot com. Thanks.

This dialogue extends the conversation to find out that the homeowner is not interested now, but will be in two years. Be sure to include your e-mail address anytime you give potential clients your telephone number. Let them decide how they want to communicate.

Calling a Friend

Calling old friends and past co-workers not only is fun, but it also can be rewarding. Friends want to help you; once they understand you are taking on real estate as your new career, they can become your live advertising, talking signs.

Salesperson: Bob, how are you?

Friend: Doing great! And you?

Salesperson: Couldn't be better. Tell you what, I'm calling to let you know about my new career with Acme Realty here in town. Since I'm new, I'd like to ask for your help to start my career off right. Can you do me a favor?

Friend: Sure.

Salesperson: If you hear of people who want to buy or sell, please give them my name. Or better yet, let me have their names, and I can call them directly. I really appreciate it.

Friend: I don't know of anyone offhand, but congratulations on your career change. I think you'll do great!

Salesperson: Thanks! With help from friends like you, I am assured of success. What about you? Have you ever thought about selling?

Friend: No, sir. I wouldn't know where to go.

Salesperson: Well, please call if I can be of service to you or if you would like a market evaluation of your home. I'll send you some of my business cards in the mail. Thanks. Good to talk to you again. Let's do something soon.

This dialogue is another great way to build your database. Follow up, follow up, and then follow up with these people, and you will cultivate a massive referral network.

Calling Someone in Your Sphere of Influence

All friends and family members are in your sphere of influence. However, they are separated here because the dialogues are a bit different. Your sphere of influence consists of all those people who know you and what you do. These people want to help you, so be sure to ask them. One student of mine took this advice, and she reported back that one of her friends was insulted because my student had never asked her for help.

Salesperson: Hello, Bob. This is Dan Hamilton with the Civic Organization. How are you this evening? As you probably know, I work with Acme Realty. The reason I've called is that I'm sending everyone in the Civic Organization a free membership in my Client Appreciation Club. It's a free services program. Membership offers discounts from many local and national companies. You also get access to me, your real estate professional, to answer any real estate questions or help you with your real estate needs. But the reason I am calling tonight is that you also receive a current market analysis of your property for your records. Do you have a second to tell me a little about your house?

You should join service organizations, clubs, and groups for the right reason, which is to serve. However, you can serve and also make the other members aware of how you make a living.

Chapter 3
For Sale By Owner Dialogues

The real estate professional who can adequately handle the "For Sale By Owner" (FSBO) can make a handsome income. For Sale By Owners believe that they can sell their property without a real estate professional. With the correct dialogue, the real estate professional should be able to convert a For Sale By Owner into a listing, sell that listing, and earn a commission from the sale. The money results from using the correct dialogue.

This chapter presents and discusses the following:

- Dialogues for calling a For Sale By Owner
- Dialogues for handling the For Sale By Owner objections
- Dialogues for Getting Referrals
- Dialogue for Stop-by

This chapter is intended specifically for real estate salespeople, real estate brokers. and managers. They will all benefit from knowing how to handle For Sale By Owners through the use of correct dialogues discussed in this chapter. Without this knowledge, these people in the real estate business are disadvantaged.

These are the objectives of this chapter:

- Understand the mentality of the For Sale By Owner.
- Know the assumptions essential for working with For Sale By Owners.
- Understand and use dialogues that will convert the For Sale By Owner into an appointment.
- Understand and use dialogues for making presentations to the For Sale By Owner.

The Mentality of the For Sale By Owner

Real estate salespeople know about For Sale By Owners (FSBOs, also known as the Fastest Source of Business Opportunities). The problem is that we don't know how to talk with them. That is the focus of this chapter—learning to talk with FSBOs

Real estate salespeople believe that FSBOs hate us. Nothing is further from the truth. Most FSBOs love us; they just don't want to pay us. Can you blame them? Would you want to pay thousands of dollars for something you believe you could do? This is the downfall of most agents. They call an FSBO and think that the FSBO is going to list that day with them. That won't happen! The FSBO still believes he or she does not need us. That's why you can benefit from dialogue designed to handle the FSBO.

How do you find FSBOs? You can find them in the newspaper, on the Internet, or simply by driving around. Finding FSBOs is not what this chapter is intended to teach. If you need to figure out how to find FSBOs, refer to *Real Estate Marketing and Sales Essentials* by Dan Hamilton.

Assumptions for Calling For Sale By Owners

There are certain assumptions that need to be made prior to calling FSBOs.

- **Assumption 1:** The FSBO believes he or she can sell the home without using a real estate professional.
- **Assumption 2:** The FSBO will eventually list with a real estate professional.
- **Assumption 3:** The real estate agent must meet the FSBO face-to-face before even beginning the process to list.
- **Assumption 4:** It is not the first agent to contact an FSBO who wins; it is the last one. As an agent, you must make every effort to follow up to ensure that you are that last agent.
- **Assumption 5:** You must be willing to continue this FSBO program each week for at least 12 weeks, or you should not bother beginning.
- **Assumption 6:** You must have a reason to call each week, and that reason should be an offer of a fair trade.

Generic Dialogue for Calling FSBOs

Salesperson: Hi. I'm calling about the home for sale?

FSBO: Yes.

Salesperson: Are you the owner?

FSBO: Yes.

Salesperson: Would you work with real estate in any way?

FSBO: What do you mean?

Salesperson: Well, my name is Dan Hamilton with Acme Real Estate, and I am going to be in your area later in the week. I was wondering if you would mind if I stopped by and took a quick look at your place?

This dialogue will get you into the homes of six of every ten FSBOs you call. Let's analyze this dialogue. In the first three lines, you have not mentioned that you are a licensed real estate salesperson. This is acceptable because the conversation has not become "substantial."

You should be careful, though, and not let the FSBO speak, because the FSBO might get excited and give you substantial information. So when you ask about the home for sale, ask the second question, "Are you the owner?" immediately, without pause. You want to find out if the person answering the phone is the owner, rather than someone, like a friend, who is helping the owner. You don't want to talk with a friend; you must talk with the owner.

The third question, "Would you work with real estate in any way?" is confusing and rhetorical. You are trying to get the FSBO's attention. Most real estate salespeople make a big announcement that they are in real estate. The FSBO is ready to reject that salesperson immediately. This dialogue allows you time to make an impression. Your response is the same no matter how the FSBO responds.

The final question is actually to solicit a "no" response. Read it again: "I was wondering if you would mind . . . ?" If the owner says no, it means he or she doesn't mind if you take a look at the property. This may elicit some laughter from the FSBO, and that is a good thing. Be sure to explain you'll only be taking a quick look. Do not vary these dialogues. They are proven.

LEGAL NOTE

Each state has some version of a "deceptive trade practices" law to protect the consumer from misleading or fraudulent business activities. It could be construed as a violation if a real estate agent made contact with a consumer and did not address the issue of licensure before the conversation became "substantial." The agent would be considered in a position of knowledge and hence in a position of advantage. A "substantial" conversation is one that becomes a negotiation or in which confidential information is exchanged.

Secondary Dialogues for Calling FSBOs

SECONDARY DIALOGUE FOR CALLING FSBOS I

This dialogue is to be used for FSBOs who are not willing from the start to let you into their home to take a quick look. Do not use this dialogue if the first dialogue works. If the FSBO says, "Sure, come on out," don't use the secondary dialogue; it is not necessary. Most FSBOs want us to come out. They think that they are getting free information, like pricing and property condition. Do not fear FSBOs; they're not that mean.

Salesperson: Is it the payment of the fee that is keeping you from listing your property with a professional real estate salesperson?

FSBO: I don't want to pay those huge commissions.

Salesperson: Well, would you mind if I sent a buyer I could not help directly to you?

FSBO: Why would you do that?

Salesperson: I'm sure you have buyers come into your home, and they end up not buying your home, don't you?

FSBO: Yeah.

Salesperson: You see, those are still potential buyers to me. If you get a list of those buyers, I would be happy trading you a buyer I couldn't help for those buyers you couldn't help. Now, doesn't that sound fair?

FSBO: Yes, I guess it does.

Salesperson: It only makes sense for me to see the house, so I will know which buyers might be interested in it. Now, I'm available tonight, or will tomorrow be better?

Again, notice that ,the dialogue continues no matter how the FSBO responds. Do not let the FSBO lead you astray. I have had FSBOs absolutely adamant that I was not getting into their house and then in the next minute, after I used the secondary dialogue, eagerly inviting me to see it.

Now, be sure you understand that you are not promising that you will give the FSBO buyers. The dialogue is careful in stating, "Trading you a buyer I couldn't help for those buyers you couldn't help." We are real estate professionals; we should be able to help all buyers. But an FSBO cannot help a buyer who is not interested in his or her particular house. On the other hand, we have an entire market of homes we could sell those same buyers.

The last paragraph of the dialogue is our reasoning for looking at the FSBO's house. It is our "stop-by" appointment and the start of our relationship with the FSBO. Some say any reason is a good reason to get into an FSBO's house. I say give a good reason and everyone wins.

On a side note, I have also received lists of buyers from FSBOs that were worth more than the one sale I would have gotten if I had listed and sold their house. Our objective is to list that FSBO, but if he or she will also give us buyers, that's an additional advantage for calling FSBOs. FSBOs have buyer lists—get them!

SECONDARY DIALOGUE FOR CALLING FSBOS II (TAKE-AWAY CLOSE)

Suppose the dialogue changes and the FSBO reacts differently to the salesperson. The following is dialogue to use in that situation:

Salesperson: It only makes sense for me to see the house, so I will know which buyers might be interested in it. Now, I'm available tonight, or will tomorrow be better?

FSBO: I don't want you in the house; you can send your buyers by, but I'm not interested in talking with agents about my house.

Salesperson: I understand you are not talking to anyone about the marketing of your house, but what we are discussing here is the aspect of working together. You send me buyers you cannot help, and I send you buyers that I cannot help. Does it make sense that I could do a more intelligent job if I did at least see the inside, so that I could excite them about your property?

FSBO: Let me tell you a little bit about it over the phone.

Salesperson: I am certain that you understand that a description you give me over the telephone is not nearly the same as an actual tour of the house. Now if you are not willing to have the buyers that I cannot help, maybe we could work together in the future?

FSBO: So you just want to take a look?

Salesperson: Yes, sir, that's correct. Now, I can come by tonight, or will tomorrow be better?

This dialogue repeats the first dialogue in another manner and follows with another question. The FSBO wants to tell about the house instead of showing, and the salesperson recognizes that the FSBO does not want to face any agents. The reason may be that he or she is vulnerable to saying yes to salespeople in person. The salesperson then gives the "take-away" close, taking away from the seller the buyers the salesperson was offering to send to the house. A take-away close is one that takes away something that the FSBO wants. Fear of loss is the greatest of motivators. As long as this technique is used honestly, it is effective. If the FSBO feels manipulated, then the technique fails miserably. Be sure to keep a steady voice and end the dialogue with a question.

Dialogue for Calling FSBOs—
Market Availability

Salesperson: Good evening. I'm Dan Hamilton from Acme Real Estate. I'm calling because I am doing an update of property available to buyers in our area. I want to be sure when I am showing buyers that they have knowledge of the entire available market. I saw the advertisement for your house. Is it available to buyers that I am working with?

FSBO: Sure, but I am not paying you a commission.

Salesperson: I understand. I can't find fault with someone trying to save money. If I had a buyer who might be interested in your home, and the buyer would pay me my commission, would you allow me to show it and sell it?

FSBO: As long as I'm not paying your for doing this, you can show it.

Salesperson: Now, doesn't it make sense for me to see the house, so I will know which buyers might be interested in your home? I'm available tonight, or will tomorrow be better?

Get the FSBO to admit to you that he or she is selling. This makes the owner commit to being interested in what you have to say.

Never talk commissions on the telephone; that discussion must wait until the seller agrees to list with you. At that time the FSBO understands your value and is willing to pay for it.

The second dialogue paragraph by the salesperson makes the FSBO admit that he or she is doing all the marketing. First it points out the burden the FSBO is taking on, and then you find out if the FSBO is currently cooperating with another real estate company. Some real estate companies will discount their fees to an FSBO if he or she does some of the work. You would not want to attempt to work with any FSBO without knowing about those types of arrangements.

In the "survey" dialogue below, you are suggesting that it is the fee that's causing the FSBO to want to sell without a professional. We know that's the reason, but we want the FSBO to tell us. I can't imagine that any FSBO would decline if we offered to help for free. However, if the FSBO says the fee is not the reason, you need to ask more questions to find out the reason.

You can use the same dialogue if you have discovered the FSBO via a sign, the Internet, or any other means.

Dialogue for Calling FSBOs—Survey

Salesperson: Hello. My name is Dan Hamilton with Acme Realty. We're doing a survey of all the owners who are trying to sell their homes without a real estate professional. Do you have a moment to answer a few questions?

FSBO: I guess.

Salesperson: Great. What is the current offering price of your property?

FSBO: I have it on the market for $218,000, which is a steal!

Salesperson: Understood. How long have you been trying to sell it?

FSBO: About two months now.

Salesperson: When you get your property sold, where will you go?

FSBO: I have a job waiting for me in Dallas.

Salesperson: Any particular time frame that you have for selling?

FSBO: I have another two months before it becomes critical.

Salesperson: Does your new job offer any transferee benefits?

FSBO: Not that I am aware of.

Salesperson: Why did you choose to sell the property yourself and not with a broker?

FSBO: To save the commission fee, of course.

Salesperson: If I were to show you how I could do all the work for you and in the end you would still save the commission fee, would you talk with me?

FSBO: How could you do that?

Salesperson: Well, if I could prove it to you, would you talk with me?

FSBO: I hate doing this, so if you could prove to me that I wouldn't lose money, I would talk with you.

Salesperson: Great. I'm available today, or would tomorrow be better?

For a survey dialogue, you should write down the survey questions in advance, but don't limit your selection. You could ask the FSBO any question you want to ask. The dialogue above gives a few critical ones. When you have the talent, the questions will flow, and a natural rhythm will ensue.

The first question is about price. Price is an easy icebreaker, but very important. If you know the area and the price the FSBO gives is well over the market value, you will quickly realize that this FSBO won't be able to sell and is prime pickin's!

The next question, "How long have you been trying to sell it?" elicits an answer that tells you how soon this FSBO may be willing to talk. The longer the house has been on the market, the better chance you have to meet with the owner. If the house is fresh on the market, it may be more difficult. Don't misunderstand: you should call the FSBO immediately, no matter if the property is fresh on the market or not. The first real estate salesperson to call the FSBO and follow up will be the salesperson the FSBO will list with. If you decide to wait, you may lose your chance.

Asking where the FSBO will be moving may set you up with a referral possibility:

Salesperson: . . . I could meet you today, or would tomorrow be better?

> ***FSBO:*** Well, I really want to try it for two more weeks. Could I call you then?
>
> ***Salesperson:*** Sure. Let me ask you, could I have someone from the Dallas area give you a call to help you on your move there?
>
> ***FSBO:*** Hey, that would be great! Thank you.

The great thing about this secondary dialogue is that it allows you more time to build rapport and the FSBO thinks you are providing a valuable service. The second great thing about this dialogue is that if the FSBO succeeds in selling the property in the next two weeks, at least you have made a referral fee!

You want to ask if there are any transferee benefits, because if you work with the FSBO's company, you may be able to provide an additional service to the FSBO and further save him or her some money.

The last thing is the statement that I can prove that the FSBO can save money by listing with me. As real estate professionals, we had better be able to prove our worth. We can negotiate better, sell the property faster, and work with ancillary businesses to save additional money. My tax accountant saves me money each year. I don't know how, and I don't care to know how. All I do know is that without him, I would have the hassle of filing taxes and I would lose money. The same should be said for us if we are truly professional.

More Generic Dialogues for Calling FSBOs

GENERIC DIALOGUE FOR CALLING FSBOS I

This dialogue is lengthy and requires an FSBO who is willing to talk. It is a very easy dialogue to use, because it works on the ability of the salesperson to talk and to think quickly.

Salesperson: Hello, is this the owner of the property advertised in today's paper?

FSBO: Yes, it is.

Salesperson: Is your house still available?

FSBO: Yes, it is.

Salesperson: Well, my name is Dan Hamilton from Acme Real Estate, and I was wondering if I could stop by and take a quick look at your house. While I'm there, I could determine whether or not I'd be able to help you sell it. Could I see it sometime this evening, or would tomorrow be a little better?

FSBO: I don't think we would be interested.

Salesperson: Just curious: the ad did not state if the house is a single-story or a two-story?

FSBO: It is a two-story.

Salesperson: Thanks. Where are you moving if you sell?

FSBO: Somewhere around Lake Colleen.

Salesperson: Ahh, nice. When do you have to move?

FSBO: We don't have to move. It is where we want to go for our retirement.

Salesperson: Understood. Again, my name is Dan Hamilton. What's yours?

FSBO: Kimberly Vinson.

> *Salesperson:* OK, Mrs. Vinson, so you are not considering using a real estate professional at this point, is that right?
>
> *FSBO:* Yes.
>
> *Salesperson:* Why is that, Mrs. Vinson?
>
> *FSBO:* We don't want to pay a commission.
>
> *Salesperson:* I don't blame you for that. If I could show you how you could have all the services a real estate brokerage could provide for you and in the end it would not cost you a cent, would you let me talk with you?
>
> *FSBO:* How could you do that?
>
> *Salesperson:* I would need to sit down with you and discuss those procedures. Now, I am available tonight, or would this weekend be better?

The dialogue above starts out with the "let me see if I can help you" close. The problem with this close is that the FSBO does not believe he or she needs help. This close does not work here either, but the salesperson is talented enough to continue the dialogue.

Next the salesperson asks if the house is a one-story or a two-story. This is a great question, because the FSBO probably has not heard a direct question like this, and it indicates the salesperson knows what buyers in that area are looking for.

The salesperson continues by asking what the FSBO will do if the property sells. With the answer, the salesperson knows that the FSBO is a candidate for a referral to Lake Colleen.

The salesperson continues asking questions until the FSBO declares it is the commission that is keeping her from listing. The salesperson then closes for the appointment by offering brokerage services and still saving the FSBO money. Remember: our services attract more buyers, and attracting more buyers gets the property sold faster at a higher price.

GENERIC DIALOGUE FOR CALLING FSBOS II

Suppose the dialogue changes and the FSBO reacts differently to the salesperson. The following dialogue may help in that situation:

Salesperson: Well, my name is Dan Hamilton from Acme Real Estate, and I was wondering if I could stop by and take a quick look at your house. While I'm there, I could determine whether or not I'd be able to help you sell it. Could I see it sometime this evening, or would tomorrow be a little better?

FSBO: I don't think so. We sold our last home in a month.

Salesperson: In this area?

FSBO: No, it was Chicago.

Salesperson: Oh, much different market. Tell me, how many people have you had through looking at your property?

FSBO: Well, we just came on the market a few days ago.

Salesperson: So let me see if I understand you right. No matter what, you are not willing to work with a real estate professional, even if I had a buyer?

FSBO: Well, if you had a serious buyer, we would work with you.

Salesperson: You would pay a commission?

FSBO: Yes, if the buyer actually buys the house, full price.

Salesperson: But you want to do all the work associated with selling the house without the use of a broker. Is that correct?

FSBO: Yes, we want to save that money.

Salesperson: If I could show you how you will lose that money anyway and still do all the work, would you let me talk to you about that?

FSBO: No, we really want to sell it ourselves.

Salesperson: How do you like selling your own home?

FSBO: I guess I don't mind.

Salesperson: So it's not taking a lot of time.

FSBO: Yeah, it does take up my free time.

Salesperson: And does that bother you?

FSBO: Of course we would rather be at the lake.

Salesperson: Let me ask you this. If I could help get you out on the lake by doing all the work for you and still not cost you more than you would pay without me, would you talk with me?

FSBO: Yes, if you could do that, I'd talk to you.

Salesperson: Let's do this. Why don't we find a time when I could stop over and take a look at your house? While I'm there, I'll do these three things for you, Mrs. Vinson. First of all, I'll show you that when we take a property, we sell it. That's a result of our marketing system. Second, while I'm there, I'll show you how I can get you more money out of your house than you can get out yourself. And third, I'll assure you that I can coordinate the sale from beginning to end so that you can buy the new home in Colleen. The end result is you're on the lake, I'm doing all the work, and you get the money. That's what you want, isn't it?

FSBO: You're going to show me how you can get me more money than I can get myself, and you're going to take care of all the details?

Salesperson: Yes. I could do that as long as you meet with me. Now, I am available tonight, or would tomorrow be better?

GENERIC DIALOGUE FOR CALLING FSBOS III

Salesperson: Hello. This is Dan Hamilton from Acme Realty. I noticed that you are selling your home yourself and wanted to call and introduce myself. The market is quite good right now, and you may be able to sell your home without a real estate salesperson. I have noticed, however, that many times people who try to sell their homes themselves eventually seek professional real estate help. I was wondering if you'd mind if I stopped by just to meet you so that, if that time comes for you, you'll feel comfortable calling me. Now, I am available today, or would tomorrow be better?

GENERIC DIALOGUE FOR CALLING FSBOS IV

Salesperson: Hi, Mr. Vinson. Dan Hamilton with Acme Realty. I drove by today, and I was a bit concerned for you. I thought maybe people weren't stopping because, well, they really don't see your sign. So I'd like to offer something that has helped a lot of my people get results. It's our For Sale By Owner sign. The size, colors, and professionalism seem to catch the eye of potential buyers. You can use it, no obligation at all. I'd like it back when you do move. Could we see how it looks? I can install it today, or would this weekend be better?

You would use this dialogue after you have made contact with the FSBO. Most FSBOs would reject this offer, but you are offering a service most other real estate professionals won't offer. Also, your contact number is on this sign and therefore always available to this FSBO.

GENERIC DIALOGUE FOR CALLING FSBOS V

Salesperson: Good morning. My name is Dan Hamilton, representing Acme Realty. I noticed your ad in the paper this morning and was wondering if you'd mind if I just stopped by to see your home?

FSBO: I would rather you wouldn't. I want to sell it myself.

Salesperson: I see. The reason I asked that question is that the ZIP code of your property is 76020, and that means you are in my direct service area. If I have potential buyers interested in your home, would you let me show it to them?

FSBO: I suppose so, yeah.

Salesperson: Wonderful. I would like to have a little bit of information about the home so that I could tell them about it intelligently. I could come by at two, or would four be more convenient for you?

FSBO: Well, I'd really rather not have you come over at this time. If you have people interested, I'd be willing to talk to them.

Salesperson: I could just send them directly to you, and you would show them?

FSBO: Yes.

Salesperson: Fine. I won't mind at all sending them to you if anyone is interested. I also have some information that we give to people who are selling their own homes to help them and prepare them for closing. I could drop by and give it to you today, or would tomorrow be better?

FSBO: Could you just put it in the mail?

Salesperson: Yes, I could do that. Again, my name is Dan Hamilton. What is yours?

FSBO: Robert Henderson.

Salesperson: Mr. Henderson, it was nice talking to you. Thank you so much for your time, and good luck on selling the home.

This time the dialogue did not get an appointment. There are no guarantees, of course, but by using the correct dialogues, you should increase your hit ratio drastically. At least this dialogue established rapport and set things up for a successful listing in the near future.

Dialogue for Calling FSBOs— Market Evaluation

Salesperson: Hi, my name is Dan Hamilton with Acme Realty here in town. May I ask you a few questions to assist me in completing a market evaluation on a similar property in your area?

FSBO: A what?

Salesperson: A market evaluation.

FSBO: Why would you do that?

Salesperson: In case I have a buyer who would be interested in your type of property, I would have the data necessary to give intelligent advice. So could I start?

FSBO: I guess.

Salesperson: Thank you. How much are you asking for your home?

FSBO: $280,000.

Salesperson: What improvements have you made to the property?

FSBO: We have replaced the carpet and updated the kitchen.

Salesperson: How many square feet are in your home?

FSBO: 3,200.

Salesperson: Any special features of your home?

FSBO: Well, we have a great view of the park with a landscaped backyard. Our garage is oversized with a work area up front, and we have one of the best lots in the neighborhood.

Salesperson: Great. And thank you. As I mentioned, I'm doing a market evaluation on similar property in the neighborhood. If you'd like, I'll share that information with you when it is finished.

> *FSBO:* Yes, I would like to see it.
>
> *Salesperson:* I should have it completed by tomorrow. I could stop by and show you that information later in the day tomorrow, or would Wednesday be better?

The FSBO is a little hesitant to give information, but by staying with the dialogue the salesperson is able to communicate with the FSBO. Offering to share market evaluation information gets the salesperson a chance to meet with the FSBO. That's of critical importance.

Handling Objections from the FSBO

The following dialogues will help the real estate professional in the answering of objections and concerns posed by different For Sale By Owner situations.

DIALOGUE FOR PRICING THE PROPERTY I

FSBO: We're asking $250,000. What do you think of that?

Salesperson: You know, I could give you a figure out of thin air. But I'm sure that's not what you want. Since you've asked, however, I will do research and compile a comparative market analysis. This will let us know at what price you should market the property. I can stop by and discuss my results with you tonight, or would tomorrow be better?

Do not give your professional advice for free. If this FSBO wants me to analyze the price and where that price fits in the marketplace, then I get a listing appointment. The next dialogue shows another version.

DIALOGUE FOR PRICING THE PROPERTY II

FSBO: We're asking $250,000. What do you think of that?

Salesperson: Well, I haven't seen the property yet, but I am available to view it and provide you feedback on pricing. Now I could come by today, or would the weekend be better?

DIALOGUE FOR AN FSBO WITH A BAD LISTING EXPERIENCE

FSBO: Eight years ago, when we sold our house, we originally had it listed with a real estate person, and she didn't do anything. She never called us; we had to call her if we wanted any information. At times I was wondering if she was still in the business. So when the listing ended, we put it on the market ourselves and sold it.

Salesperson: Did she hold an open house?

FSBO: Once.

Salesperson: How did that go?

FSBO: I don't know. She never called!

Salesperson: Did she advertise it?

FSBO: I assume she did.

Salesperson: How do you like selling your own home?

FSBO: I don't mind.

Salesperson: So, it's not taking a lot of time?

FSBO: Well, sure.

Salesperson: Does that bother you?

FSBO: If you are asking if I would rather be playing golf, the answer would be yes.

Salesperson: Let's do this. Let me come over and take a look at your house and see if I feel I can help you. While I'm there, I could show you how I could get you out on the golf course by doing two things. Number one, getting you the most money in the shortest amount of time, and number two, guaranteeing that if you put me to work for you, I'll get the job done. Does that make sense?

FSBO: Yes, it does.

Salesperson: I can stop by today, or would the weekend be better?

Some FSBOs have had a bad experience. Let them vent, and then you can begin by asking questions to defuse their anger.

DIALOGUE WHEN YOU HAVE A QUALIFIED BUYER

FSBO: Do you have a qualified buyer?

Salesperson: It depends. I haven't seen your home yet. I can come by and look at your property today, or would tomorrow be better?

The close for the appointment is quick and powerful. If the FSBO asks this type of question, you should be ready with this direct response.

DIALOGUE FOR AN FSBO WHO WON'T PAY A COMMISSION I

FSBO: I won't pay a commission, so there's no reason for you to come out.

Salesperson: If I find a buyer and I can build my professional service fee into the price of your home, so you get the net amount of money you need, will you be willing to work with me and allow me to show your property?

FSBO: I guess so.

Salesperson: Now, I would like to take a look at your property today, or would tomorrow be better?

DIALOGUE FOR AN FSBO WHO WON'T PAY A COMMISSION II

Salesperson: Is the main reason you're not wanting to let me look at your property the fee? And I hope you'll be honest and candid. Is that the reason?

FSBO: That's it. I can sell it myself and save the money.

Salesperson: So in other words, if I were doing it for free, you'd let me serve you?

FSBO: I guess so, but you can't do that.

Salesperson: In essence, I am working for you for free.

FSBO: What do you mean?

Salesperson: You see, the main reason you are selling your home on your own is to avoid paying the brokerage. The main reason that a buyer avoids professional real estate service is to avoid paying the same brokerage. Two people can't save the same brokerage. Does that make sense?

FSBO: Yes, but why do you say you work for free?

Salesperson: Buyers shop For Sale By Owners only for a discount, or they would be looking at all available properties on the market. So to sell your home, you will have to give the buyers a discount on the price somewhere around the fee you would have paid me. Now, if you are going to pay that amount to a buyer as a discount or to me as a fee, which do you feel will help you more?

FSBO: I don't care as long as I get my home sold.

Salesperson: But you need to think this through. The buyers do not give you anything and still take that money. I, on the other hand, will represent you and will do all the marketing on your home, which frees up your time and saves you hundreds of dollars on marketing costs. Do you see the advantage of having me work for you? Now, I am available to come take a look at your house today, or would tomorrow be better?

DIALOGUE FOR AN FSBO WHO WON'T PAY A COMMISSION III

FSBO: We need every cent we can get from the sale to put down on our new house. You see, we can't afford to pay a real estate commission.

Salesperson: Understood. If I could show you how you possibly could make as much, or maybe even more, and let me handle all the work and negotiations, would you meet with me?

DIALOGUE FOR AN FSBO WHO IS TIRED OF AGENTS CALLING

FSBO: I'm so sick of real estate agents calling me! Do you know how many have called me today?

Salesperson: You know, you are fortunate for that. If there wasn't a tremendous market for your home, no agents would be calling. That makes sense, doesn't it?

From here the salesperson simply begins asking questions, as in the above dialogues. Do not challenge the FSBO.

DIALOGUE FOR AN FSBO WHO HAS JUST LISTED

FSBO: I'm sure we'll get a buyer in no time. We've only had the house on the market one week and already three people have come to see it.

Salesperson: Were they qualified to buy?

FSBO: Well, I assume so.

Salesperson: Do you know why a significant amount of buyers want to only look at houses on the market For Sale By Owners?

FSBO: I assume to save a little money.

Salesperson: True, but some realize they can't qualify to buy a house. Real estate professionals won't show them listed properties, so they resort to viewing properties For Sale By Owners to dream of the day when they can buy. Great for the buyers, but not much for you. Would you like the buyers who come through your house to be qualified to actually buy it?

FSBO: Well, sure.

Salesperson: Let me come by and discuss this with you. I am available now, or would this evening be better?

DIALOGUE FOR AN FSBO WHO CAN DO THE SAME AS YOU

FSBO: What do I need you for? I can put up a sign in my yard just like you would.

Salesperson: True. And you could spend hundreds of dollars buying that sign, placing advertisements, and holding open houses. Or you could let me do all that work for you, and you would end up with the same amount of money in your pocket when you sell. Would you let me have the chance to explain? I could discuss this with you later on today, or would tomorrow be better?

DIALOGUE FOR AN FSBO WHO HAS A FRIEND IN THE BUSINESS

FSBO: If I list my property, it will be with my friend in real estate.

Salesperson: That's great! It's an advantage to have a friend in the real estate business. Could I ask his or her name?

FSBO: Why?

Salesperson: So if I have a buyer for your property, I will already have a relationship with your agent.

FSBO: Well, you can work directly with me until then.

Salesperson: If you wish, I can stop by and look at your place today, or would tomorrow be better?

FSBO: For what?

Salesperson: To determine if I have any buyers who would be interested in a place like yours. We could meet now, or would this weekend be preferable?

Sometimes the FSBO will claim to have a friend in the real estate business to throw you off. If you ask for the name and the FSBO won't reveal it, you can assume there's no such friend. In this dialogue, the salesperson immediately assumes then that the FSBO will let him or her in to see the house. When the FSBO hesitates, the salesperson gives a response and again assumes that the meeting will take place.

DIALOGUE FOR AN FSBO WHO IS NOT SHOWING THE HOUSE TO SALESPEOPLE

FSBO: We're not showing our house to real estate salespeople.

Salesperson: I understand how you feel. What you're saying is that you're not willing to pay a commission. Is that true?

FSBO: That's true.

Salesperson: I see. Let me ask you, when I'm showing houses to potential buyers in your neighborhood and they ask about your home, would you mind my giving them the information?

FSBO: No, please tell them about it. We will pay you a buyer's fee!

Salesperson: Great. Then I'll need to see the home in order to tell them about it effectively. What time would be better, five o'clock or seven o'clock this evening?

Dialogues for Getting Outbound Referrals

DIALOGUE FOR GETTING OUTBOUND REFERRALS I

This dialogue is for those real estate agents who want a different reason to call FSBOs. Do not call FSBOs about the property they're selling, but call them about their next real estate purchase. This angle allows you to make contact without putting the FSBO on the defensive. One other benefit: you may actually make money on the outbound referral, once the FSBO sells and moves.

Salesperson: Hello. My name is Dan Hamilton, the relocation specialist of Acme Real Estate Company.

FSBO: Yes?

Salesperson: I'm not calling about your home. But I'd like to know, when you sell it, are you staying in the area, or will you be relocating out of town?

FSBO: We'll be relocating to the Dallas area.

Salesperson: That's great! Would it be helpful to have housing information for that area before you go to Dallas?

FSBO: Sure.

Notice I am not saying that I am a Nationally Certified Relocation Specialist, only that I am the relocation specialist for my office.

DIALOGUE FOR GETTING OUTBOUND REFERRALS II

Salesperson: Hello. My name is Dan Hamilton, the relocation specialist of Acme Real Estate Company.

FSBO: Yes?

Salesperson: I am not calling about your home. But I'd like to know, when you sell it, are you staying in the area, or will you be relocating out of town?

FSBO: We will be relocating to the Dallas area.

Salesperson: Great! I thought you might be interested in our referral service. A lot of people who sell their own homes have taken advantage of it. Through our referral network group, I can get information on areas, home prices, local points of interest, mortgage rates, and much more to you within a couple of days. There is no cost or obligation on your part. May I have one of our group members contact you?

This dialogue is a different angle for talking with an FSBO. Once the FSBO has given you all the information about where he or she is moving, you should say:

Salesperson: Fine. I will have someone on this immediately. Now that I have you on the phone, could I ask, how are you doing with selling your property?

By expressing concern about the person's move, you have earned the right to ask about his or her house. You should now move that forward with a request to look at it.

Salesperson: I see. I tell you what—I would love to come take a look at your property and maybe give you some good suggestions that might make the marketing process easier on you. Now, I am available today, or would tomorrow be better?

You are back to making an effort to get the listing. You have the referral in hand, and the FSBO likes you. At the end you use a close like the one in the *Alternate Choice Dialogue* as presented in Chapter 1 to ask for the appointment.

DIALOGUE FOR GETTING OUTBOUND REFERRALS III

Salesperson: Hi. My name is Dan Hamilton with Acme Realty, and I noticed that your house is currently for sale.

FSBO: How can I help you?

Salesperson: I'd like to offer you free relocation services. May I ask, when your house sells, where will you be moving?

FSBO: Dallas.

Salesperson: Great. Please share with me the area of town and your housing needs so that I may contact our relocation department and get you some specific information that could help you.

DIALOGUE FOR GETTING OUTBOUND REFERRALS IV

Salesperson: Hi. My name is Dan Hamilton with Acme Realty, and I noticed that your house is currently for sale.

FSBO: How can I help you?

Salesperson: I would like to offer you free relocation services. May I ask, when your house sells, where will you be moving?

FSBO: We will be moving across town and getting a bigger house.

Salesperson: So you are not moving out of the area. May I ask, will you be needing the services of a professional real estate agent in finding another property?

FSBO: I suppose so, when the time comes.

Salesperson: I represent buyers and would be willing to give you some information on the areas where you are looking now so you will have a better idea of what it will take to move. Would this be of interest to you?

Dialogue for Knocking on an FSBO's Door

One of the best ways to get into an FSBO's house is to approach the door unannounced. This is tough on the real estate salesperson, but it is very effective. An FSBO is quick to tell you no over the telephone, but it is much more difficult in person. The following is a dialogue to use.

Salesperson: Good afternoon. My name is Dan Hamilton with Acme Real Estate. I just wanted to stop by and give you a picture of your house. (Hand him or her the picture.) I've found that many people sell their home without ever having a picture of it. I think the picture came out great, don't you?

FSBO: Yes, thanks.

Salesperson: While I am here, I was wondering if you mind if I just took a quick look at your place?

This technique gives the FSBO something of value and creates an obligation for him or her to give you something back in return. What you want is the opportunity to view the house. You can take the photo digitally and then print it on quality photo paper; then place it in a quality sleeve with your contact information. Doing it this way gives you the opportunity to show your professional image and that you care about doing things right. Just handing over a snapshot is not effective. Last, do not give a reason to take a look. Ask and you will usually be allowed in. If the FSBO insists on a reason, you should use the *Secondary Dialogue for Calling FSBOs* presented earlier.

Dialogues for an FSBO Stop-By

DIALOGUE FOR AN FSBO STOP-BY I

The FSBO stop-by should be just that—a stop-by. As soon as you get a stop-by appointment with the FSBO and hang up the telephone, you should put a note in the mail reminding him or her of the date of the appointment and enclose a business card. Include an agency disclosure form if required by local laws.

Take a notebook and a pen—that's all. You said this is a stop-by appointment. Do not take a briefcase or any other listing material. You should have everything needed to list the property in your car, but you should leave it there. If the FSBO wants you to list the house, you will be prepared—but only if the FSBO wants you to do so.

Once inside the house, you should use the following dialogue.

Salesperson: If you will, please show me through and just treat me as if I were a buyer.

If the FSBO says something about the house, you write it down. If it's important enough for the FSBO to say, it's important enough for you to write down. Work hard to develop rapport with the seller by asking the following questions:

Salesperson: May I ask why you are selling?

Salesperson: To where will you be moving?

Salesperson: When do you have to arrive at your new location?

Salesperson: Would you mind sharing with me the things you are doing to market your home? Maybe I can make some suggestions that will help you.

Salesperson: May I show you the things that we do to market properties?

Salesperson: How did you choose your asking price?

Salesperson: If you were to list, do you have an agent in mind? Why him/her?

Salesperson: If I could show you how my services would cost you little or nothing, would you consider listing your home with me?

If the FSBO does not seem interested in answering any questions, simply view the house and leave. You can continue to develop rapport later through follow-up.

DIALOGUE FOR AN FSBO STOP-BY II

This dialogue would be used with an FSBO after the real estate salesperson has made contact. This dialogue is for following up.

Salesperson: Hi, Mrs. Vinson. Dan Hamilton with Acme Real Estate again, on my way to do some additional business, and I wanted to check in. I thought, you know, you might have someone interested in your home, and you may not know all the documents required to sell a property. So I put some of the documents together for you, if you would let me just go over them with you. It is rather confidential, however. Could I come in and show you?

FSBO: I am not listing with you.

Salesperson: I understand, but if I help you tonight, you may find it in your heart to help me sometime in the future, isn't that correct?

FSBO: Certainly.

Once inside and seated at the kitchen table, you continue this dialogue:

Salesperson: Mr. and Mrs. Vinson, the first document we will discuss is the One to Four Family Residential Contract (Resale). It is also called an Earnest Money Contract, a Purchase Agreement, and a Sales Contract. This is what documents the sale, the contract you and the buyer sign to bind the transaction. I'd suggest getting a large earnest money deposit. Do you know what an earnest money deposit is?

FSBO: Isn't that the good-faith money from the buyer?

Salesperson: That's correct. The larger the deposit, the better it is for you. Now the next form is the Addendum for Sales of Other Property by Buyer. This addendum allows the buyer the right to tie up your property while still making an effort to sell his or hers. Do you have a problem with a buyer for your house while he or she still has a house to sell?

FSBO: No, the buyer must have cash or at least a bank loan and be ready to buy.

Salesperson: Understood, but I have to tell you everything. The next form is the Buyer's Temporary Lease. This lease allows the buyer to move in prior to closing. This helps out those buyers who need a place to stay immediately. Do you have a problem with moving out so a buyer could move in prior to closing?

FSBO: No way!

Salesperson: OK, OK, don't shoot me; I am only the messenger. Sounds to me that maybe you should have someone on your side protecting your position. I could go on discussing the forms, or you could hire me and let me worry about all of this stuff and still get you out with just as much money, if not more. Just say yes.

According to the *National Association of Realtors® Profile of Home Buyers and Sellers*, difficulty with paperwork was the second biggest problem FSBOs had in selling their homes.

Dialogues for Making a Presentation to an FSBO

DIALOGUE FOR MAKING A PRESENTATION TO AN FSBO I (SOMEONE NOT INTERESTED)

Salesperson: Mr. and Mrs. Vinson, I clearly understand your interest in selling your property without using a real estate professional in an effort to save the commission, but I would like to share with you some things that you may want to know. First of all, you should know that owners of real estate have been hiring real estate professionals like me for several hundred years. That is a long time. Would you agree that there must be value in working with a real estate professional or our business would have faded away years ago?

FSBO: Yes, I suppose.

Salesperson: The second thing you should know, Mr. and Mrs. Vinson, is that 70 percent of For Sale By Owners like you end up selling their homes with some help from a real estate professional like me. Were you aware of that?

FSBO: No, not really.

Salesperson: The third thing you should know is that real estate professionals like me are able to sell a property for a higher price in a shorter period of time than an owner could. Would you like to know why?

FSBO: Yes, but we're still not going to list with you.

Salesperson: Understood. There are several reasons everything I have said so far is true. Let me explain why. The first reason is that buyers shop for For Sale By Owner homes only in order to save money. Basically, the buyer is looking to discount the price; the discount is usually the same amount as a commission. By the way, you mentioned that saving the commission is the reason you are trying to sell your house yourselves. Wasn't that what you said earlier?

FSBO: That's correct.

Salesperson: Mr. and Mrs. Vinson, let's think this through. We are assuming that buyers are going to look for only For Sale By Owner properties. Why do you think they would do that?

FSBO: It would give them a better deal.

Salesperson: Exactly! That is the same commission you are trying so desperately to save. Two parties cannot save the same commission, agreed?

FSBO: Of course.

Salesperson: So if push comes to shove, who do you think will save the commission, you or the buyers?

FSBO: I'm sure the buyers would.

Salesperson: Sadly, it is true. Furthermore, what services will the buyers give you for the money they are going to save?

FSBO: Nothing!

Salesperson: Again, I agree with you. Which would you rather do—pay a real estate professional like me the commission and get all my services, or pay a buyer and get nothing?

FSBO: With those two choices, I would rather pay you, but if I get a buyer and I have to pay that buyer the commission, at least I got a buyer!

Salesperson: True. And that brings me to my next point. How will you generate buyers?

FSBO: We have a yard sign, and I have run a couple of newspaper ads. My son is going to put up a Web site featuring our home, when he gets around to it.

Salesperson: In the real estate industry in this area, we have approximately two thousand real estate professionals. Suppose each of these agents has at least five buyers that he or she is working with currently. This means that we have about ten thousand potential buyers who could be interested in your home at this very moment. Can you see that with ten thousand prospective buyers right now, we professionals are more likely to sell your house for more money in less time than you possibly could?

FSBO: Yes, I could see that.

Salesperson: The last point I would like to make is that most of the buyers going through your home are not actually qualified to buy it. Some don't know how to get qualified, and others are just looky lous who wouldn't take the house if you gave it to them. How do you currently qualify a buyer who wants to view your home?

FSBO: We don't.

Salesperson: Interesting. Do you see the liability and concern I would have for you just letting anyone who wants come though and look around?

FSBO: Hadn't thought of it that way. I haven't felt uncomfortable, though.

Salesperson: But you certainly could be wasting your time. Would you agree with that?

FSBO: Yes, I feel I am doing a great deal of that.

Salesperson: We are continually trained to be able to qualify a buyer before he or she enters your home. This qualification may limit the number of lookers, but it will not limit the number of buyers. Do you see the advantage of having a real estate professional such as me pre-qualify each and every buyer?

FSBO: Yes, that is important.

Salesperson: I feel, Mr. and Mrs. Vinson, you should know these things. Now, doesn't it make sense to put me to work for you?

DIALOGUE FOR MAKING A PRESENTATION TO AN FSBO II (SOMEONE INTERESTED)

FSBO: Well, we have some people interested.

Salesperson: You have some people interested? Great! Do they seem pretty interested?

FSBO: They have been by twice!

Salesperson: Let me ask you this: if these buyers weren't interested, then would you have listed with me?

FSBO: Yes, I am sure we would have.

Salesperson: Let's do this. Let's go ahead and put the home on the market and exclude these buyers from our listing agreement. That way if they buy, you owe me nothing, but in case they don't, we are not wasting marketing time. Does that make sense?

This dialogue sets it up nicely. The salesperson acts as if he or she is not going to get the listing and then offers a solution that would be hard for the FSBO to overcome.

Chapter 4
Expired-Listing Dialogues

One of the biggest fears of real estate professionals is having a dialogue with a homeowner with an expired listing. These homeowners are some of the best and easiest to work with if the correct dialogues are used. This chapter addresses the expired-listing homeowner and how to have effective and productive dialogues with him or her.

This chapter presents and discusses the following:

- Dialogues for calling and for stopping by an expired-listing homeowner to develop business
- Dialogues for answering any objections the expired-listing homeowner would have
- Dialogues for extending the conversation with the expired-listing homeowner to aid in building rapport with him or her

This chapter is intended for the real estate professional who wants to increase his or her sales and total production. The expired-listing homeowner is not for the brand-new real estate salesperson without the correct dialogues because these homeowners have been lied to by a so-called real estate professional in the past. The previous real estate professional declared that he or she could sell the property and did not deliver. When you call, the homeowner believes you are the same. The correct dialogue will enhance the conversation and calm the homeowner down so that an intelligent conversation can continue.

These are the objectives of this chapter:

- Be able to list and discuss the assumptions in working with homeowners with expired listings.
- Understand the mentality of expired-listing homeowners and what they are seeking in their next real estate professional.
- Understand and be able to use dialogues to call homeowners with expired listings and communicate your professionalism to them.
- Be able to list the five things that it takes to sell a house and how to use them in dialogues.
- Understand and be able to use dialogues to handle any objections that homeowners with expired listings would have.
- Understand and be able to use the Property Qualification Sales Forecaster.

The Expired-Listing Homeowner

Expired listings are those for which the agent did not do his or her job and sell the property. Notice, I said the agent did not do his or her job. You cannot blame the market, the sellers, or the president if your listings expire. You could have refused to take it if you believed you could not sell it. If you discovered you could not sell it and had already agreed to the listing, you could have released it.

Too many real estate salespeople take a listing just to get a listing, no matter whether the listing is salable or not. There are many reasons why you might take a listing, including the following:

- Your broker harps constantly, "Get the listing!"
- All the other salespeople have a listing, and you have none.
- You haven't had a listing in months.
- You think having a listing makes you busy.
- You believe you can always get the owner to lower the price later.
- You know you have competitors and hope that by claiming you can get the seller a higher price, he or she will list with you.
- You at least generate calls from buyers and can move them to better properties.

No matter what your excuse, if you take a listing that you know is unsalable, then you are manipulative and will have a difficult time in this business.

Assumptions for Calling Expired Listings

When calling on expired listings, the real estate professional should know the following assumptions:

- **Assumption 1:** Homeowners of expired listings want to sell. They've proved it by trying to market the property.
- **Assumption 2:** Homeowners of expired listings don't have a problem paying a commission. Again, they've proved it by signing a listing agreement to pay.
- **Assumption 3:** Homeowners with expired listings don't hate agents—but be aware that they hate that their property has not sold, and they may not like their current agent, so they may take it out on you.
- **Assumption 4:** It is best to be one of the first to call. A

homeowner of an expired listing may make appointments with only the first two or three agents who call. Also, be persistent. If you do not reach the owner on the first call, call until you do.

■ **Assumption 5:** Keep the homeowners on the telephone as long as possible. The longer you extend the call, the more relaxed the owner becomes, the more he or she realizes the need to sell, and the more he or she acknowledges that it was not you who caused the problem.

How to Find Expired Listings

This book is not intended to help you find expired listings, only to convert the ones you find into current listings by using the correct dialogues. To find out how to reach an expired listing, check with your broker. Also, there are many books available that discuss the procedure. Each particular area will have its own methods for reaching the expired-listing homeowners.

Dialogues for Calling on Expired Listings

DIALOGUE FOR CALLING ON EXPIRED LISTINGS I

Once you have located the contact information of an expired-listing homeowner, you should call him or her immediately. The National Do Not Call Registry rules apply, so be sure to follow them. If you cannot call or cannot find the phone number, you should drive over to the property and knock on the door. The dialogues are virtually the same for either approach. Phoning is faster, and knocking is more effective. How about doing both? The following dialogues will help convert an expired-listing homeowner call into an appointment.

Salesperson: Mrs. Vinson?

Expired: Yes.

Salesperson: This is Dan Hamilton with Acme Realty. I am calling about the property on Colleen Court.

Expired: Yes?

Salesperson: Is that property still for sale?

Expired: No.

Salesperson: Well, I'd like to stop by and take a quick look at the place and, while I'm there, tell you why your property did not sell. So if you decide to put it back on the market, the same mistakes won't be made again. Does that make sense?

First, you want to establish you are talking with the right person. Most Multiple Listing Services include the owner's name on each listing. You then want to establish that you are calling on the expired-listing property. The last initial question you want to ask is about whether the property is still listed for sale. You know it is not, but you want to find out whether the owner knows that or not. If, as in the above dialogue, the homeowner knows the property listing has expired, you now know that the homeowner is informed in some manner. Maybe the former listing agent has called. Maybe several other agents wanting the listing have called. All you know is that the homeowner is aware. If, as in the following dialogue, the homeowner is not aware of the listing expiring, you know the homeowner has not been told and you are the first agent to call.

DIALOGUE FOR CALLING ON EXPIRED LISTINGS II

Salesperson: Mrs. Vinson?

Expired: Yes?

Salesperson: This is Dan Hamilton with Acme Realty. I am calling about the property on Colleen Court.

Expired: Yes?

Salesperson: Is that property still for sale?

Expired: Yes.

Salesperson: Did you know that it has been taken off the computer system?

Expired: No.

Salesperson: Yes, I guess your listing with your current agent has expired. I tell you what I would like to do: I'd like to stop by and take a quick look at the place and, while I'm there, tell you why your property did not sell. So if you decide to put it back on the market, the same mistakes won't be made again. Does that make sense?

Here the homeowner did not know her listing had expired. The only way this would be possible is if the listing agent had not communicated with the owner. It is amazing to me how many real estate professionals do not communicate with their bosses (the homeowners). We promise to do our best, and then we can't find the time to call? That makes no sense to me. The number-one complaint of any expired-listing homeowner is, "The agent put a sign in the yard and a key box on the door, and it was the last time I ever spoke with him [or her]." Don't be that type of agent. Call your homeowners at least weekly.

Notice that in the dialogue, I say the property had been taken off the computer system and do not use the word "expired." Most homeowners could figure out what "expired" means here, but all understand about a computer system. I don't want to confuse the homeowners in any way.

Both dialogues end with a trial close of "Does that make sense?" You would further ask for the appointment using an alternate choice close, such as the following.

Expired: I guess so.

Salesperson: Great! I can be over there today at six o'clock, or would eight o'clock be better?

DIALOGUE FOR CALLING ON EXPIRED LISTINGS III

Salesperson: Good morning, Mr. Vinson?

Expired: Yes.

Salesperson: I am Dan Hamilton with Acme Realty. I'm calling because your listing is shown on our computer as having expired. Have you relisted the property?

Expired: No.

Salesperson: Are you still interested in marketing your home?

Expired: Yes, but I may sell it myself.

Salesperson: May I ask why you are moving?

Expired: I'm being transferred to Dallas.

Salesperson: I hope that is a good thing?

Expired: Yes, it's a promotion.

Salesperson: Well, congratulations!

Expired: Thank you.

Salesperson: Mr. Vinson, did you know that there are five reasons why a home either sells or does not sell?

Expired: No. I don't know real estate that well.

Salesperson: Understood. The first and most important reason is the price you ask for the home. Do you feel your offering price is reasonable?

Expired: For my house, yes, but it is better than most in the neighborhood.

Salesperson: I see. Well, the second factor is if you can offer the buyers any terms or incentives to help them get into the home. Did you offer to carry the financing for the buyer or offer to pay the buyer's closing costs?

Expired: Well, no. Isn't that the buyer's responsibility?

Salesperson: Could be. The third factor is the actual condition of the property. Mr. Vinson, is the property in good shape?

Expired: Like I said, it is the best property in the area.

Salesperson: Right, you said that. The fourth factor is the location of the property, both locally and nationally. Not much we can do here, but the location will affect price. And the fifth factor is the marketing that is done to get your home sold by your real estate agent. Do you agree with those factors?

Expired: Makes sense.

Salesperson: Which of these reasons do you think caused your home to not sell?

Expired: I would assume it was the marketing.

Salesperson: Agreed. And did you further notice that the only one you do not have control over is the location? I guess what I am saying, Mr. Vinson, is that you chose the agent to do your marketing. But because the agent did not do the things necessary to sell the home, you are left without a sale. Does this make any sense to you?

Expired: Yes, I can see that.

Salesperson: So don't give up on selling your home, and don't give up on real estate professionals. Just select the best one, and let him or her work for you. Mr. Vinson, did you know that I believe in my services so much that I will guarantee them to you?

Expired: No. What do you mean?

Salesperson: Let me stop by and look at your property, and maybe I can determine what went wrong last time and then show you what I can do. Also, at that time I will show you my guarantee of service so that you can feel assured you have hired the right real estate professional. Now, I can be by today at three o'clock, or would five o'clock be better?'

Expired: Five o'clock would be best.

Salesperson: Great! See you then. One other thing, Mr. Vinson. You will be getting a slew of these calls today, so you may want to take your telephone off the hook so you won't be bothered.

> ***Expired:*** Thanks. See you at five.

This dialogue demonstrates the effectiveness of extending the conversation as long as possible. This real estate professional did that by asking lots of questions. Let's go over this dialogue in detail.

The agent first determines that the homeowner knows his property is off the market and does not want to continue selling with a real estate professional. This is actually good news. This homeowner will eliminate every other real estate salesperson who calls. This homeowner will not relist because he is not happy with his former agent. Some homeowners will relist because they feel the agent did a good job, but the market would not allow the home to be sold. These homeowners are tough to get. However, this one would be easy because he is so unhappy that he is going to do it himself. Now, you do not have to overcome the other agent; you just have to prove you can sell the property.

The next thing the agent does is to change subjects and ask the homeowner why he is moving. This takes the homeowner's focus away from the fact that his home did not sell and moves him to think about the objective, to get moved.

The agent then describes the five things that it takes to sell a home:

- Price
- Terms
- Property condition
- Location
- Marketing

The expired-listing homeowner will always blame the

marketing; that certainly is a factor, but the usual culprit is the price of the property. Almost anybody can sell a property if it is priced right; the market does that. Good marketing simply exposes that property to more people in a shorter time. No amount of marketing could sell a property that is extremely overpriced.

The homeowner begins to warm to the agent, so the agent closes by discussing his or her guarantee. Any real estate professional can and should offer a guarantee. It simply states, "If I do not do what I promise, you can fire me." Shouldn't that be part of your service? I think so. This real estate professional is smart enough to brag about it. By offering a guarantee to an expired-listing homeowner, you give that person the confidence that you will do your job; and if not, he or she does not have to endure another round of inadequacy and can fire you. I have never been fired for doing my job even if the home didn't sell. The key to not being fired is communication. If you communicate with the homeowner about your activities, then he or she will be happy with your service. If you do not communicate, you should be fired!

The agent then follows that with the alternate choice close for the appointment.

DIALOGUE FOR CALLING ON EXPIRED LISTINGS IV

Salesperson: Hello, is this Mr. Vinson?

Expired: Yes. Are you in real estate?

Salesperson: My name is Dan Hamilton, and I am with Acme Realty. I'm calling because your listing has been taken off the market. I am really sorry your home did not sell.

Expired: Me too.

Salesperson: So you still want to sell it, then?

Expired: I have to. Our next home is being built, and I can't afford two house payments!

Salesperson: I see. Not a good situation. We have found that when a home on the market has not sold, there are a variety of reasons. Would it help you if you could determine exactly why your home did not sell?

Expired: Yes, I would be very interested.

Salesperson: We have an exclusive Property Qualification Sales Forecaster that will isolate what it is that caused your home not to sell. It is a very accurate written analysis of every possible reason a home will or will not sell. With our Property Qualification Sales Forecaster, we can determine the weak areas of marketing and determine how to exploit those areas to get your home sold. Does this sound like something that you might be interested in seeing?

Expired: Yes.

Salesperson: I could show it to you now, or would this evening be better?

The real estate salesperson again first determines the homeowner's desire to sell the home. The salesperson continues by offering the Property Qualification Sales Forecaster. This is simply a sheet of paper with questions on it to help determine the marketability of the property. This forecaster is also helpful in determining the flexibility of the homeowner. Each item on the list that the property has will mean the property is more salable. You could create one yourself, but here is an example, which you can modify if you wish.

Property Qualification Sales Forecaster

Marketability Item	Yes	No
List at or below retail price		
Owner financing available		
Low down payment (if owner-financed)		
Below-market interest rate (if owner-financed)		
Government terms available (FHA, VA)		
Post-dated price reduction		
Sale price at break point		
Full-term listing agreement		
Above-normal fee for service		
Easy access (key box, no prior notice)		
Yard sign installed		
Homeowners to redecorate/remodel (if necessary)		
Immediate possession		
Trade terms/lease available		
Extras included (appliances, swing set, etc.)		
Pre-order appraisal		
Pre-order inspection report		
Home protection plan ordered		
Avoid contingencies (buy first, not until school is out, etc.)		
Available for first tour		
Homeowners to complete necessary repairs		
Homeowners acknowledge the Property Qualification Sales Forecaster		

This forecaster is to be customized for your needs and your area; this is simply an example. Let's review each item on the list so that you will have the dialogues necessary.

List at or below retail price—The price must be set at or below the market value, or the house will not sell.

Salesperson: The property must be priced right to sell, do you agree?

Owner financing available—This item shows the flexibility of the homeowner. It also expands the pool of buyers for the property. If the homeowner would finance, many more buyers would be interested.

Salesperson: Could you offer financing to the buyer?

Low down payment—If the homeowner would consider financing, would he or she accept a low down payment? Some homeowners would finance with 25 percent down. That large down payment will eliminate any would-be buyers. If the owner will finance and accept a low down payment, then the market opens up to many more potential buyers.

Salesperson: Now that you have agreed to consider financing, would you accept a low down payment?

Below-market interest rate—This one works the same as the one above. If the homeowner could finance at an interest rate lower than the market rate, it would open up the property to more offers.

Salesperson: Now that you have agreed to consider financing, would you allow the buyer an interest rate that is below the current rate?

Government terms available—Some homeowners demand cash and accept nothing else. They believe that "cash is king." Demanding cash could also eliminate most buyers.

Salesperson: Would you allow a buyer to put an offer to you using government financing, such as FHA or VA financing?

Post-dated price reduction—The homeowner agrees to reduce the price sometime in the future by signing a Post-Dated Price Reduction form. All you have to do is use a standard Price Reduction form and post-date it.

Salesperson: To keep buyers interested in your home, we should agree to adjust the price periodically. To do that, I have with me a Post-Dated Price Reduction form. All I need is your acknowledgment right here.

Sale price at break point—Buyers buy at certain price breaks, yet real estate agents price property like we're selling cereal or gasoline. I have never heard buyers tell me, "We are looking between $187,454 and $194,977." That's not how they buy. The buyers say, "We are looking between $185,000 and $195,000." We should price our properties with the same reasoning. For example, if we list a property at $189,999 to look clever, instead of listing at $190,000, look what happens:

	List Price = $189,999	$190,000
If buyer price break is $180–$190, will the property be shown?	✓	✓
If buyer price break is $185–$195, will the property be shown?	✓	✓
If buyer price break is $190–$200, will the property be shown?	NO	✓

Notice that for $1 the listing agent has missed a potential price break. Price property in the same way as buyers think.

Salesperson: We should price your property at even price breaks, such as $190,000. Is that fine with you?

Full-term listing agreement—I have no idea what the listing term should be in your area, but if the average number of days on the market is 120, you had better not take listings of 90 days!

Salesperson: With homes in this market selling in approximately 120 days, do you agree to have your home exposed to that market for six months?

Above-normal fee for service—Again, I have no idea what you charge as your commission, but this is one way to ask for more. I believe you can ask for more only if you are worth it. However, if the homeowner gives you more, could you offer some or all of the difference to the buyer's agent and possibly get more showings?

Salesperson: Normally we charge a certain fee for service, but do you see the benefits to you by providing additional funds that could be used as incentives for the buyer's agent?

Easy access—If a homeowner makes access to the property more difficult, he or she could miss out on potential showings and potential sales.

Salesperson: Mr. and Mrs. Vinson, do you see why it's so important to have a key box on your property?

Yard sign installed—It is amazing to me that some homeowners do not even want a yard sign. Your job is to sell them on the fact that a yard sign is important.

Salesperson: A yard sign can generate as much as 8 percent of the sales of houses. It would be a shame to miss out on that market segment. Could we put up a sign within the next two days?

Homeowners to redecorate/remodel—Some houses need extensive repairs and updating. If the homeowner is unwilling to fix up the property, he or she must be willing to reduce the property significantly. Even with a price adjustment, some buyers cannot see what the property could look like and refuse to make an offer.

Salesperson: Mr. and Mrs. Vinson, we discussed how the house needs updating—things like the carpet and painting. Could we have the remodeling completed within two weeks?

Immediate possession—If a homeowner wants to stay in the property for a few days after closing, certain buyers see that as a problem. The buyers may be renting and must have a place to stay when their lease ends. If they are unable to take occupancy at closing, this factor could be enough to force the buyers to choose another property.

Salesperson: I understand it will take a while to get your stuff out of the house, but if it is necessary, could we begin the move early enough to be out by closing?

Trade terms/lease available—If the homeowner is willing to consider a trade of house for house or willing to lease the house for a few months, that flexibility will open up the property to additional buyers.

Salesperson: Would you ever consider leasing this property for a short time if we had a legitimate buyer?

Extras included—If the homeowner would consider leaving the refrigerator or lawn equipment, these things that mean a great deal to a first-time homebuyer could be enough to swing the deal and really not give up much on the sales price.

Salesperson: Could we include the refrigerator in the sale if the price is right?

Pre-order appraisal—A real estate professional could determine the price for the home, but an actual appraisal carries more weight with a buyer and could give the buyer confidence that the price asked is correct.

Salesperson: If we were to order an appraisal report today, then we would know what price to set, and the buyer would feel confident that the price is accurate. Could we order one today?

Pre-order inspection report—The same reasons as above.

Salesperson: If we were to order an inspection report today, then we would know what repairs would be required to sell, and the buyer would feel confident that your property has been maintained well. Could we order one today?

Home protection plan ordered—A home protection plan helps everyone in case of a problem with any main aspect of the house. If the owner agrees to provide a protection plan, the agent can promote it as a selling point.

Salesperson: Mr. and Mrs. Vinson, do you know what buyers fear most in purchasing a home?

Homeowners: No, not really.

Salesperson: They are afraid that after they buy the home, something will go wrong, and they will have to pay to have it fixed. Basically, that they will have bought a lemon. Do you two know the most frequent cause of lawsuits involving real estate?

Homeowner: No.

Salesperson: The same thing. Someone buys a house and the air conditioner breaks, so the buyer sues everyone. The one way for you to avoid having to defend against such a claim is to order a home protection plan that would cover such difficulties. Do you see the importance of ordering a home protection plan?

Avoid contingencies—Any contingencies that the homeowner places on the sale of the home would make a sale more difficult.

Salesperson: I understand that you want to wait till your son graduates, but if we get a full-price offer on your property before that, would you ever consider selling?

Available for first tour—Some homeowners want to wait till the "right" time to have their home toured by the office. If the homeowner waits too long, the "new on the market" aspect of the property wears off, and the agents in the office are not excited to see it.

Salesperson: We have our office tour next Thursday. Could I go ahead and put you down on that specific tour date?

Homeowners to complete necessary repairs—If there are any repairs needed, it takes time to complete them, and the house will show poorly without them. Get the homeowner to complete them before the house goes on the market.

Salesperson: So you will have the two windows replaced and the back door fixed by the first of next week. Is that correct?

Homeowners acknowledge the Property Qualification Sales Forecaster—This just ensures that the homeowner knows you are serious about the forecaster.

Salesperson: Mr. and Mrs. Vinson, all I need is your acknowledgment of the forecaster to be sure that we are on the same page with the marketing and sale of your property.

Finally, notice that all the dialogues assume that the homeowner will list with you. Do not ever say, "If you list...." Just assume that the homeowner will list.

More Dialogues for Calling on Expired Listings

DIALOGUE FOR CALLING ON EXPIRED LISTINGS I

Salesperson: Hello. Is this Mrs. Vinson?

Expired: Yes.

Salesperson: My name is Dan Hamilton with Acme Realty. Did you sell your home, or is it still available?

Expired: It is still available.

Salesperson: Were you aware that it was taken off the market this morning?

Expired: No, I wasn't.

Salesperson: Are you still interested in selling?

Expired: Yes. Do you have a buyer?

Salesperson: I can't determine that until I have a chance to see it. And that is the reason I called: to see if I can stop by, take a look at your house, and ask you some questions that will help our marketing department. While I'm there, I can give you a net sheet that would help determine how much money you will walk away with when you sell your home. May I stop by tonight at six o'clock, or would eight o'clock be better?

When the homeowner asks if the salesperson has a buyer who is interested, the salesperson evades that question by maneuvering for an appointment to visit the property and talk about how much money the homeowner could receive.

DIALOGUE FOR CALLING ON EXPIRED LISTINGS II (RELISTED)

Salesperson: Is this Mr. Vinson?

Expired: Yes.

Salesperson: My name is Dan Hamilton with Acme Realty. I

see in the Multiple Listing System that your listing has expired. Have you relisted your home?

Expired: Yes.

Salesperson: Have you actually signed the papers to relist?

Expired: We signed them last night.

Salesperson: Great! Can I ask, for how long did you put it back on the market?

Expired: For 30 days.

Salesperson: Could I call you back near the end of that time and see how things are going?

Expired: I hope it is sold by then, but yes, you can call me then.

Salesperson: Agreed. Thank you.

In the dialogue above, the homeowner has signed papers, but only for 30 days. In the real estate business, 30 days is a blink of the eye. Then I ask if I can call him back near the end of the time. The owner agrees. I now have permission to call before the property expires again. I got that permission because I had the right to call. Never let your listings expire, or you may lose them. Check with local customs, regulations, and guidelines to be sure this action holds up in your area.

Most agents will stop as soon as they find out that the owner has listed the property. If the owner has not yet signed the papers to relist, do your best to get a chance to list the property before the owner signs with another agent. Be sure your local regulations allow this; most do. Use this dialogue.

Salesperson: How long did you have it listed last time?

Expired: Six months.

Salesperson: Six months! Don't you think that was long enough to give the agent a good chance?

Expired: The market is bad.

Salesperson: Is it? Anyway, here's what I can do for you. I could come out there and give you an idea as to why it did not sell the last time, so if you choose to sign the relist papers with your current agent, some of the same mistakes won't be made the next time. Does that make sense?

Some real estate salespeople think this dialogue is a little aggressive. I agree, but if the other agent let the listing expire, I now have the right to call. I believe I am the best real estate salesperson for the owner. And if you believe that you're the best, then you need to call and give the homeowner a chance to sell his or her property through you—the best!

DIALOGUE FOR CALLING ON EXPIRED LISTINGS III

Salesperson: Mr. Vinson?

Expired: Yes.

Salesperson: This is Dan Hamilton with Acme Realty. I am calling about the property on Colleen Court.

Expired: Yes.

Salesperson: Is that property still for sale?

Expired: Yes.

Salesperson: Did you know that it has been taken off the computer system?

Expired: Yes, I think the agreement ran out yesterday.

Salesperson: Why do you think your property did not sell?

Expired: I think the market is bad right now.

Salesperson: Most people believe it's the market or the agent, when in fact it's the price and the marketing. Did you know that homes are selling every day?

Expired: Not from what I have been hearing.

Salesperson: A lot of those news stories are from other places and not here. You know, I was asking myself why your home didn't sell, and I think the secret is in the answer to this question: how many people did your previous agent personally contact each day to get your home sold?

Expired: What do you mean?

Salesperson: What actions did your agent take to sell your home—or in this case, to not sell it?

Expired: I am really not sure. The last agent never called. If we wanted information, we had to call her.

Salesperson: I am sorry to hear that. Mr. Vinson, it's vitally important for you to understand the different marketing approaches if you're thinking of interviewing more agents for the job of selling your home. So let me ask you, do you know the difference between passive and active marketing?

Expired: I guess not.

Salesperson: Passive marketing is when actions are taken and then the buyer will contact the salesperson. Passive marketing would include things such as holding open houses, sending out flyers, or advertising in the newspaper and on the Internet. Did your last agent do any of these things?

Expired: I'm not sure. Probably.

Salesperson: Active marketing is going out and finding potential buyers. Active marketing would include such things as phoning as many people as possible every day and asking them if they would like to buy your home or if they know someone who would like to buy your home.

Now, which way, passive or active, do you believe will get more homes sold?

Expired: Well, active would.

Salesperson: Exactly. And you understand that what I am doing right now is active marketing? This call proves that I do what I say I will. So when would be a good time for me to come over and tell you how Acme Realty and I can get your home sold in the least amount of time and for the most money? I am available at six o'clock, or would eight o'clock be better?

This dialogue uses the contrast between active marketing—prospecting—and passive marketing. Homeowners want their agent to actively go after buyers, but most agents market passively. This dialogue points out that difference and gives the homeowner the option of hiring a real estate professional who promises to market actively.

Asking Extension Questions

The key thing in dealing with an expired-listing homeowner is to extend the conversation as long as possible. The longer you can keep a homeowner on the telephone, the better off you will be. Expired-listing homeowners are angry that their home did not sell, but they are not angry with you. The longer you can keep an expired-listing homeowner on the telephone, the more rapport you will build and the more the homeowner will trust you. The reason for these questions is to extend the conversation and the contact. Ask these extension questions:

- Is your house still available?
- Why do you think your house did not sell?
- What do you believe the previous company did that helped you the most to market your home?
- What do you feel your previous company should have done to sell your home?
- Did your previous company advertise regularly?
- Did you ever have an open house for the public?
- What were the comments of the buyers who looked at your home?
- Why are you moving?
- What is your time frame? When do you have to have the house sold?
- How long have you lived in the home?
- Have you made any major improvements to the home in the last year?
- Would you consider carrying any of the financing for the buyer?

- Are you talking with any other real estate company about selling your home?
- You were asking $280,000 for the house. How did you arrive at that price?
- Do you have any concerns in making a move?
- What is the most important to you—the price you get, the length of time it takes to sell, or the convenience of getting the property sold?
- What would it do to your plans if you just couldn't sell?
- Can you move first without selling the home?
- How did you happen to choose that company?
- What type of Internet marketing was used?
- Was there a virtual tour?
- What electronic mailings were done to promote the property?
- Did you receive any offers during your listing period?

If you let the homeowner describe the challenges, you will get ideas about the marketing systems and strategies that he or she wants. It is in answering these questions that homeowners reveal their frustrations, concerns, and complaints about their experiences with real estate professionals. These questions also qualify the homeowners and enable you to decide whether you want to pursue obtaining this listing.

Objections from Expired-Listing Homeowners

Expired-listing homeowners will have objections at times. Here are a few dialogues that can help:

DIALOGUE WHEN OTHER AGENTS HAVE CALLED

Expired: You've got a lot of nerve! You must be the tenth real estate agent who's called me.

Salesperson: Actually, I was notified today that your property is not on the market. But what did the other brokers want?

Expired: To list my house!

Salesperson: Well, that's not why I'm calling. I called because I am confused about why it did not sell. What do you think was the reason it did not sell?

This dialogue defuses the homeowner's frustration. The property was listed for six months and hardly anyone called, and today it expires and five or six real estate agents call—and it seems like ten or twenty. The salesperson then begins to ask questions and extend the conversation.

DIALOGUE WHEN PROMISES WERE BROKEN

Expired: I don't like real estate agents because they tell you all the great things they will do and then don't do any of them! We are very disappointed!

Salesperson: I don't blame you there. Why do you feel your home didn't sell?

Don't try to make excuses about the other salesperson. Just agree and then move on. Again, ask questions and extend the contact.

DIALOGUE WHEN THE HOMEOWNER ASKS ABOUT BUYERS

Expired: Do you have a buyer?

Salesperson: I don't know. I haven't seen your house yet.

Handle this objection the same way every time. Don't defend yourself; you haven't seen the house, so you could not possibly know if you have a buyer. You could close now to make an appointment to look at the property, or you could ask questions and extend the contact.

DIALOGUE WHEN THERE WAS NO ADVERTISING

Expired: The previous company never advertised this house. Will you advertise every week?

Salesperson: I can't know what marketing is needed on your property until I see it.

The question is different here, but your response should be the same as in the preceding dialogue: you need to visit the property.

DIALOGUE WHEN THE HOMEOWNER ASKS ABOUT LACK OF INTEREST EARLIER

Expired: Why didn't you bring a buyer around when it was on the market the last time?

Salesperson: Well, I was not aware your house was listed. You see, an agent should let all the other cooperating brokers in your area know that your house is on the market through other efforts besides the Multiple Listing Service. Frankly, I don't know now if any of my buyers would be interested in your house, because I haven't seen it yet. I could come on over and take a look at your property now, or would three o'clock be better?

Expired Listings—Special Situation Dialogues

DIALOGUE FOR CALLING A NEIGHBOR OF AN EXPIRED LISTING

This dialogue is designed for calling on a neighbor of an expired listing. Neighbors may have the information you need to contact the homeowners. If you can get this information, it is like gold because most other agents won't have it.

Salesperson: Good morning. My name is Dan Hamilton, and I am a real estate professional with Acme Realty. Recently, I discovered that your neighbor's home at 1234 Colleen Court has been taken off the market, and I cannot find any information on the owner. Do you happen to know how I can contact the homeowner?

Neighbor: No, I don't know the homeowner.

Salesperson: There has been a lot of activity generated in this area because your neighbor's house is on the market. Have you or anyone you know thought of selling, either now or in the near future?

The last part of the dialogue shifts from the property in question to prospecting for other properties to list. Hey, if you have a potential client on the telephone, there's no harm in asking.

DIALOGUE FOR CALLING AN AGENT BEFORE THE LISTING EXPIRES

Suppose you've noticed a listing with a competitor that has very little activity for the last few months. You know this because you drive by it frequently. You may want to call that competitor and use this dialogue.

> *Salesperson:* Is this Nathan Scott?
>
> *Other Agent:* Yes.
>
> *Salesperson:* My name is Dan Hamilton, and I am with Acme Realty. I've noticed the property at 1234 Colleen Court has been on the market for 80 days. I was wondering if we could partner together to get that property sold?
>
> *Other Agent:* What do you mean?
>
> *Salesperson:* If you introduce me to your sellers and get your broker to transfer the listing to me, I will give you a referral fee, and you won't have to be concerned about that listing anymore. I am an expert in that area. Sometimes a new agent can make all the difference for the seller, and after 80 days, something for you is better than nothing.

Gutsy technique, but I like it. It sometimes takes courage to make it big in real estate.

The first thing about this dialogue is that you must be aware of the days on market for listings. Keeping track of that for all the listings on the Multiple Listing Service would be very difficult. I suggest using this technique for properties in your farm area (i.e., the part of town you focus on) or ones with which you are quite familiar.

Call when a listing reaches 80 days. Don't wait any longer. Some agents list properties for 90 days; if you wait till then to call, it may already be expired. If the agent has listed it for six months, he or she will reject you unless it is not going well. Remember: we cannot call the homeowner and ask if it is going well, as this is an ethics violation, but we can call the listing agent and ask that question.

You may think that if the listing agent is not happy with

the homeowners, he or she will refer that listing in-house. But there are two things to consider. First, the agent probably has not thought about that and will react positively to your question. In smaller firms the agent may be able to convince the broker to transfer the listing. (Only brokers can transfer listings.) If you are talking with the broker, then he or she can transfer the listing without a problem. Of course, the homeowner must agree, but it's your job to convince him or her that you are the best agent to handle the listing. The second thing is that both the agent and the broker may understand that no one else in the company is qualified enough to handle a homeowner who feels frustrated or angry. It may be best for the agent and broker to wash their hands of this listing and move on. As a broker, I can tell you there have been plenty of times when I would have transferred a listing to a competitor just to get rid of a rude homeowner—but no competitors asked for the listing.

DIALOGUE FOR CALLING AN AGENT AFTER THE LISTING EXPIRES

You call the agent after the listing has expired only if you cannot find contact information for the homeowner. If you have the contact information, there's no reason to use this dialogue.

Salesperson: Is this Nathan Scott?

Other Agent: Yes.

Salesperson: My name is Dan Hamilton, and I am with Acme Realty. I noticed the property at 1234 Colleen Court has been taken off the computer system.

Other Agent: Yes, it expired today.

Salesperson: Are you going to relist that home?

Other Agent: No.

Salesperson: If you would give me the owner's name and contact information, I will give you a referral at closing. How does that sound? At least you get something from your efforts.

Other Agent: The owners are not negotiable.

Salesperson: If you give me their contact information, I will take it from there. If I cannot do my job and get the listing, you still haven't lost anything. Does that make sense?

Other Agent: Yeah, I guess.

As mentioned before, sometimes an agent and a homeowner do not see eye to eye. Because of this, they don't get the property sold. Once a new salesperson enters the scene, some homeowners become much more negotiable.

Chapter 5
Business Development
Door-to-Door Dialogues

Real estate professionals have generally had negative feelings about door-to-door marketing. They believe that consumers do not like this type of marketing. There is nothing further from the truth. The people who hold that belief do not know the types of dialogues that are effective in door-to-door marketing. With the correct dialogues, not only is door-to-door marketing effective for making money, but it is also fun!

This chapter presents and discusses the following:

- Dialogues for door-to-door marketing
- Dialogues for answering any objections the homeowner may raise

This chapter is intended for the real estate professional who wants an additional source of income. This chapter will help that individual by providing appropriate dialogues and directions for using them.

These are the objectives of this chapter:

- Understand the positives and negatives of door-to-door marketing.
- Understand and be able to use dialogues in door-to-door marketing.
- Understand and be able to use dialogues for handling objections from homeowners.

Door-to-Door Marketing for Business

Door-to-door marketing (door knocking) has been ridiculed as not something a professional real estate person would do. But times have changed, and it's now again the new way to market. The National Do Not Call Registry is making telephone calling more difficult, but there's no "Do Not Knock" list. Now many real estate professionals are using door-to-door marketing as a source of new business.

Door-to-door marketing is simply going around knocking on doors to see if homeowners have thought about selling. Remember that 5 percent of all homeowners move every year. Getting out there and knocking on doors will result in activity— and activity leads to money. When you knock and the door opens, use the dialogues in this chapter.

Dialogues for Door-to-Door Marketing—General

DIALOGUE FOR DOOR-TO-DOOR MARKETING— GENERAL I

Salesperson: Hi. I just wanted to take a few moments to introduce myself. My name is Dan Hamilton with Acme Realty. I am the residential specialist in this area. Here's my card. Please feel free to call me any time should you have any real estate questions or needs. Thanks a lot, and have a great evening! Oh, by the way, have you considered selling your home now or in the near future?

Homeowner: Not at this time.

Salesperson: Well, keep me in mind if you ever do.

This dialogue is simple and to the point. You introduce yourself and your company and tell why you're there. You hand the homeowner a business card and get ready to leave. Then you add, "Oh, by the way," and ask the question that matters most—"Have you considered selling?" You can use this dialogue when prospecting in your farm area or in other areas.

DIALOGUE FOR DOOR-TO-DOOR MARKETING— GENERAL II

Salesperson: Hi. I just wanted to take a few moments to introduce myself. My name is Dan Hamilton with Acme Realty. I am the residential specialist in this area. Here's my card. Please feel free to call me any time should you have any real estate questions or needs. Thanks a lot, and have a great evening! Oh, by the way, have you considered selling your home now or in the near future?

Homeowner: Well, yes, we have.

Salesperson: When would that be?

Homeowner: Actually, right away. My husband and I were just talking about it.

Salesperson: When would be a good time for you, your husband, and me to get together so that I may show you how Acme Realty and I can help you sell your home in the least amount of time and for the most money?

When the homeowner answers the big question positively, you shift the dialogue to asking for an appointment.

DIALOGUE FOR DOOR-TO-DOOR MARKETING—GENERAL III

Salesperson: Hi. I just wanted to take a few moments to introduce myself. My name is Dan Hamilton with Acme Realty. I am the residential specialist in this area. Here's my card. Please feel free to call me any time should you have any real estate questions or needs. Thanks a lot, and have a great evening! Oh, by the way, have you considered selling your home now or in the near future?

Homeowner: Not for another year.

Salesperson: As a real estate professional, I see homes every day in this area, and I know what it takes to market your home to get it sold. I would be more than happy to share with you some premarketing ideas, so that in a year we will be much more prepared. Can you see how that will help?

Homeowner: That would be great.

Salesperson: I will need to get some things from my office. I am available later today, or would tomorrow be better?

This response is the one you will get most frequently. The homeowner is interested, but not for a year. You would want to keep in touch with this homeowner until he or she is ready to sell. Use the pre-marketing technique to create urgency for the homeowner to meet with you.

DIALOGUE FOR DOOR-TO-DOOR MARKETING—GENERAL IV (JUST FOR FUN)

Sometimes door-to-door marketing can be challenging. Try this technique, just for fun! Choose a neighborhood, and begin going door-to-door. Have a co-worker do the same in another neighborhood. The two of you plan to go door-to-door for maybe two hours and then meet up somewhere. Use the general dialogue presented earlier.

Salesperson: Hi. I just wanted to take a few moments to introduce myself. My name is Dan Hamilton with Acme Realty. I am the residential specialist in this area. Here's my card. Please feel free to call me any time should you have any real estate questions or needs. Thanks a lot, and have a great day! Oh, by the way, have you considered selling your home now or in the near future?

Once both of you have completed your door-to-door marketing and met as planned, switch areas: you do his area and he does the area you just covered. Use the following dialogue.

Salesperson: Hi. I just wanted to take a few moments to introduce myself. My name is Dan Hamilton with Acme Realty. I am the residential specialist in this area. Here's my card. Please feel free to call me any time....

Homeowner (interrupting): A guy from your office just stopped by and said the same thing.

Salesperson: Oh, really, who was that?

Homeowner (taking out the card): Bob Johnson.

Salesperson: Wow, are you kidding? Bob is the best! If Bob wants to market your home, then you are in the best hands. Congratulations, and have a great day!

Now you have helped Bob. This homeowner thinks Bob is interested in his property and that must be good because Bob is the best! It's fun to watch the reaction of homeowners. You may want to skip some of the houses. If so, then when you and Bob meet, he can give you the addresses where he talked with the homeowners. This is not something you would want to do regularly, because it is more time consuming, but it's fun! Of course, if you can talk your co-worker into doing the same for you, homeowners in the first area will think you're the best, too.

Dialogues for Door-to-Door Marketing—Survey

DIALOGUE I

Salesperson: Hello. My name is Dan Hamilton from Acme Realty. I stopped by to introduce myself and to apply for the job of being your real estate consultant.

Homeowner: I don't want to sell at this time.

Salesperson: Understood. I would just like to ask a couple of questions, if I may. How long have you lived in this home?

Homeowner: About eight years.

Salesperson: What made you choose this neighborhood?

Homeowner: The trees and the quiet. It is so quiet at night, we just loved it!

Salesperson: How do you feel about the growth taking place in this neighborhood?

Homeowner: I am not sure that there has been much growth, but I think it has been stable.

Salesperson: I see. Do you have plans to move again anytime in the future?

Homeowner: Well, maybe in three or four years, but if it does-n't happen, we will just stay here.

Salesperson: Do you have any ideas how we can make this neighborhood better?

Homeowner: I think speed bumps should be installed to slow the cars down in this neighborhood. There are children playing near the streets, you know?

Salesperson: Understood. I will certainly make a note of your suggestion. Do you have any real estate needs or questions?

Homeowner: No, not at this time.

Salesperson: Fine. It was nice talking with you. And if you would put my business card on your refrigerator, I am right there handy if you ever have any real estate questions. Thanks again.

This dialogue turns your visit from an introduction into a survey. A survey is great when you're talking with people who are responsive, but few are this responsive. People in general feel that they are too busy to answer surveys. When is the last time you filled in or answered a survey? For most people the answer is never. If you can get people to answer your survey questions, whatever information you collect is very valuable, so the effort is worth it.

DIALOGUE II

Salesperson: Hi. My name is Dan Hamilton with Acme Realty, and I am conducting a market survey to establish projections for the upcoming year. Would you please help me by answering a few questions?

Homeowner: Yes, I guess.

Salesperson: Great! Thank you. How long have you lived here?

Homeowner: Eleven years.

Salesperson: Wow, that's quite a while. Do you feel the area is improving or declining?

Homeowner: I would say it's been about the same over the last several years.

Salesperson: Do you feel the shopping facilities and school systems are adequate for this area?

Homeowner: Yes. I don't necessarily like shopping here, but there are enough grocery stores and department stores.

Salesperson: Are you satisfied with the local school system?

Homeowner: I suppose so. You know, our children are grown, but some of the neighbors have children and they seem happy.

Salesperson: What is the most important thing that keeps you in this area?

Homeowner: It is near my husband's work.

Salesperson: Have you ever thought about moving?

Homeowner: Not until my husband retires, and that isn't for several years.

Salesperson: What changes do you feel are needed in our local government?

Homeowner: Oh, I'm not much into that. I suppose it will take care of itself.

Salesperson: Is there anyone in your neighborhood who might be less fortunate than you and me who could use our help?

Homeowner: Gosh, no, I don't think so, but it's mighty nice of you to ask.

Salesperson: Great! In a couple weeks this survey will be completed, and I'll get back to you with the results. Thank you very much, and have a fabulous day!

By offering to bring back the results, you now have set another meeting with this owner. She may have thought about moving, but now you have pushed it to the front of her mind. Suppose she discusses the idea with her husband and you show up a few days later with the results of your survey. Her attitude has become positive.

Dialogues for Door-to-Door Marketing— Specific Person

DIALOGUE 1

Salesperson: Hi. I just wanted to take a few moments to introduce myself. My name is Dan Hamilton with Acme Realty. I am the residential specialist in this area. Here's my card. I've been showing property to some clients of mine, the Hendersons, who are interested in this area but have been unable to find exactly what they want. And I wondered, have you considered selling your home now or in the near future?

Homeowner: Yes, we have talked about it.

Salesperson: When would be a good time for you and me to get together so that I may preview your home for my clients and, of equal importance, show you the value of your home and how Acme Realty and I can help you sell it? I am available later this afternoon, or would this weekend be better?

This dialogue uses a specific person, a client, as the reason for the visit. You must have the client, but that's not difficult. Suppose you have some buyers named Henderson. You have shown them a couple of houses, but they did not like them. After you show them around, ask them this question:

Salesperson: Mr. and Mrs. Henderson, could I call the area and ask the homeowners if they would want to sell? This way I may be able to find you a home faster. May I do that?

So you now have your buyers, your reason for knocking on doors. Also, think of how your clients feel about you, calling around a neighborhood for them! What a nice person!

DIALOGUE II

Salesperson: Hi. I just wanted to take a few moments to introduce myself. My name is Dan Hamilton with Acme Realty. I am the residential specialist in this area. Here's my card. I've been showing property to some clients of mine, the Hendersons, who are interested in this area but have been unable to find exactly what they want. And I wondered, have you considered selling your home now or in the near future?

Homeowner: Why? What are they interested in?

Salesperson: Have you considered selling?

Homeowner: Maybe. What do your buyers want?

Salesperson: They are more interested in this area than anything specific in a house. I think once they walk into the right home in this area, they will know it. They are pre-qualified and ready to buy. Could I come in and make notes of the property to discuss with them?

Homeowner: How much are they qualified for?

Salesperson: Well, of course you realize that is confidential information. Have you thought about how much you would want to ask for this property?

Homeowner: I know I need to walk away with at least $100,000 in my hand.

Salesperson: Great! That gives us a start. Now could you show me through and give me an idea as to why you bought this house?

In this situation, with a homeowner who's inquisitive, even suspicious, persistence is the key to getting inside. Once inside, the salesperson can ask lots of questions and build rapport.

In the first part of the dialogue, the homeowner evades the question, "Have you considered selling your home?" The salesperson persists with the question. If you cannot get an answer to this question, the homeowner can later say, "Well, we don't want to sell."

This salesperson does not answer the homeowner's question about what the Hendersons want, because the answer could have given the homeowner a reason to dismiss the salesperson. Whether the Hendersons would actually like the house or not is not the issue. Getting into the house, building rapport, and eventually listing the property is the goal.

The salesperson does not answer the homeowner's question about how much the Hendersons have qualified for, because the answer could have prompted the homeowner to want more. The salesperson would have lost the opportunity to work with this homeowner.

Dialogues for Door-to-Door Marketing— Specific Property

DIALOGUE I

Salesperson: Hi. I just wanted to take a few moments to introduce myself. My name is Dan Hamilton with Acme Realty. I am the residential specialist in this area. Here's my card. I am currently marketing a property in this area on the corner of Allen Avenue and Brittany Boulevard. I was wondering if you might know of someone thinking about moving into this area who might be interested in that property?

Homeowner: No, I don't.

Salesperson: Because of our marketing efforts, we are having a lot of interest in this area. Have you ever thought about selling?

In this dialogue, a specific property is used as the reason for the visit. The first question is important only to set up the real question, "Have you ever thought about selling?"

DIALOGUE II

Salesperson: Hello. I'm Dan Hamilton with Acme Realty. I am passing through the neighborhood today to let you know that I am marketing a home on the corner of Allen Avenue and Brittany Boulevard, just down the block. I wanted to let you know about the home just in case you know someone who would like to live in this area. Can you think of anyone who is planning to move?

Homeowner: Well, maybe my sister and her family.

Salesperson: Great! Can I get her name and number and invite her and her family to see the property?

Homeowner: Her name is Amber Adams, and her cell number is 817-555-1212.

Salesperson: Thanks for that. Here's a flyer about the property just in case you think of anyone else. My contact information is on the bottom. By the way, the market is particularly strong right now. I wonder, have you considered moving?

Homeowner: No, we love it here.

Salesperson: That's good to hear. I will contact your sister right away and see if I can't get her into this neighborhood too.

If the homeowner mentions anyone who might be interested, you should ask for the name and number of the person. Never trust the homeowner to give that person your number—it won't happen.

DIALOGUE III

Salesperson: Hello. I'm Dan Hamilton with Acme Realty. I am passing through the neighborhood today to let you know that we sold the property on the corner of Allen Avenue and Brittany Boulevard, just down the block. I also wanted to let you know that we generated a great deal of buyer interest and was wondering if you or anyone else in this area has talked about moving?

Homeowner: No, I'll probably live here till the day I die.

Salesperson: I understand. It was nice talking to you.

You will not get somewhere with every homeowner you visit. If there is no interest, move on—it's a numbers game.

Dialogue for Door-to-Door Marketing— Choose Your Neighbor

Salesperson: Good evening. I'm Dan Hamilton with Acme Realty. I'm here tonight representing the Hendersons down the street, who are selling their house and leaving the neighborhood. This is an opportunity for you to have a friend or family member move close to you. Do you know anyone that you would like to have live in the neighborhood?

Homeowner: No, I don't think so.

Salesperson: We will be generating a lot of activity in the area. Have you ever thought about selling your house?

This dialogue gives you a legitimate reason to knock on this homeowner's door: he or she may know of someone wanting to move into the area. While you're there, you should ask if the homeowner is interested in selling.

Dialogue for Door-to-Door Marketing— Help Me

You should use this dialogue if you know your neighbors well.

Salesperson: Bob, how are you? I'm stopping by to let you know about my new career with Acme Real Estate here in town. Since I'm new, I'd like to ask for your help to start my career off right. Can you do me a favor? If you hear of anyone who wants to buy or sell, would you let me know?

Neighbor: Sure.

Salesperson: Thanks. I'd really appreciate it. What about you? Have you ever thought about buying investment property?

Neighbor: Maybe, but not now.

Salesperson: Well, please call if I can be of service to you. Or if you would like a market evaluation of your home, just let me know. Here is a business card. Nice talking with you. Thanks.

It is good to get your friends helping you. They want to help, so let them. It is always best to talk with them in person, and this dialogue is the best to use.

Dialogues for Handling Objections

You should use the following dialogues to handle any objections that could come up while marketing door-to-door.

DIALOGUE WHEN THE HOMEOWNER REBUFFS SOLICITATION I

Homeowner: Please don't bother me anymore. I don't like to be solicited.

Salesperson: I understand your concern. You don't want to be bothered by strangers or solicitors coming to your door. However, I'm not soliciting. I'm offering a service to this neighborhood and plan to keep people informed of real estate values, market conditions, and other neighborhood concerns. If you'd rather I didn't stop by, could I keep you informed by mail or e-mail? Would that be of interest to you?

You would use this dialogue if the homeowner reacts negatively, but could still be interested. Some homeowners are suspicious of strangers at their door, so understand their resistance but don't let it stop you.

DIALOGUE WHEN THE HOMEOWNER REBUFFS SOLICITATION II

Homeowner: Did you know it is not allowed to solicit in this neighborhood?

Salesperson: I presume that you think I am soliciting, but I am not. I'm offering a service to this neighborhood and plan to keep people informed of real estate values, market conditions, and other neighborhood concerns. If you'd rather I didn't stop by, could I keep you informed by mail or e-mail? Would that be of interest to you?

In this situation, the homeowner rebuffs the visit with a reason, but you respond in the same way as in the preceding situation.

DIALOGUE WHEN THE HOMEOWNER HAS A FRIEND IN THE BUSINESS I

Homeowner: If I sell my house, I will use my friend.

Salesperson: I understand. Let me ask you, how soon will you be putting your home on the market?

Homeowner: Not for at least three years.

Salesperson: Tell you what, could I stay in touch with you and give you market updates? That way, when it comes time to sell, you will be more informed.

This homeowner will not be selling for a while. By staying in touch with this homeowner, you are setting yourself up for the listing. The other agent probably won't be in the business in three years; and even if so, his or her follow-up procedures are not as good as yours.

DIALOGUE WHEN THE HOMEOWNER HAS A FRIEND IN THE BUSINESS II

Homeowner: If I sell my house, I will use my friend.

Salesperson: I understand. Let me ask you, how soon will you be putting your home on the market?

Homeowner: Sometime in the next three months.

Salesperson: What I would like to do for you is to meet with you and give you some information that will help you sell the house. You can use this information in conjunction with any information your friend will give you. All I need to do is take a quick look through and then do a little work for you. Is it convenient for me to look through now?

Homeowner: Well, like I said, I have an agent, and I don't want you to do all that for me without getting paid.

Salesperson: I appreciate that, but I am more concerned about you. You see, getting only one view of the real estate business and how to sell property limits the marketing that can and will be done on your property. If you allow me to give you additional information, you will have a greater spectrum of opportunities to sell your house. Could you show me through and let me help you?

Homeowner: Why would you want to help me if I am going through another real estate professional?

Salesperson: Because I believe that helping others in some way always helps you. If you will let me help you, somehow, somewhere, somebody will help me. Now all you need to do is show me through. Could we do that?

This homeowner is much tougher, but well worth the effort because he or she will be selling soon. Again, once inside the house, you build rapport and then set up a meeting to discuss listing the house with you. Do your best to get the listing appointment before the homeowner meets with the other agent to list because there might not be a chance afterwards. The competition for this listing is fierce, but it's well worth trying.

DIALOGUE WHEN THE HOMEOWNER IS CURIOUS ABOUT THE TIMING

Salesperson: Hi. I just wanted to take a few moments to introduce myself. My name is Dan Hamilton with Acme Realty. I am the residential specialist in this area. Here's my card. Please feel free to call me any time should you have any real estate questions or needs. Thanks a lot, and have a great day! Oh, by the way, have you considered selling your home now or in the near future?

Homeowner: Yes, but how did you know?

Salesperson: We do a lot of business in this area, and activity is strong. I was just working this area and took a chance that you might want to sell. Now, do you have a second to show me through your house?

The homeowner is shocked by the timing of your visit and your question, because her husband just got a job transfer and last night they discussed selling the house. She was about to find a real estate company, and suddenly you show up at her door. Don't let her surprise throw you off. Door-to-door marketing is most effective when the timing is right.

DIALOGUE WHEN THE HOMEOWNER WON'T OPEN THE DOOR I

Homeowner: Who is it?

Salesperson: My name is Dan Hamilton with Acme Realty.

Homeowner: I am not interested.

In this situation, I recommend the knock-and-leave technique. Don't waste your time here. This homeowner is not interested, and it's good to know that immediately so you don't waste your time.

DIALOGUE WHEN THE HOMEOWNER WON'T OPEN THE DOOR II

Homeowner: Who is it?

Salesperson: My name is Dan Hamilton with Acme Realty.

Homeowner: What do you want?

Salesperson: If you would open the door, I could explain my presence.

Homeowner: I don't open my door to strangers.

Salesperson: I am not a stranger. I am a real estate professional specializing in this area. (Hold your card up to the peephole.)

or

Salesperson: I am not a stranger. I am a real estate professional specializing in this area. If you would open the door a crack, I could slide you my card.

If the homeowner is hesitant, but seems less closed than the door, you may end this dialogue in this way.

Salesperson: It seems to me you are extremely nervous about opening the door, so I will leave my card and some information about my company. I will be in the neighborhood for a while; so if you want to track me down or give me a call, we could meet later. Thanks for now.

Chapter 6
Dialogues for Working with Sellers

This chapter presents dialogues for talking with sellers prior to a listing appointment, dialogues for making the presentation, and dialogues for working with the sellers after taking a listing. Dialogues with sellers could take up many books, so in this chapter we will discuss the dialogues that are most important.

This chapter presents and discusses the following:

- Dialogues prior to attending a listing appointment
- Dialogues for making a listing presentation
- Dialogues for handling questions and objections from sellers
- Dialogues for post-signing discussions

This chapter is designed for the real estate professional that believes in listings and how to have dialogues with those seller clients. This chapter should help the real estate professional in taking listings and getting those listings sold.

These are the objectives of this chapter:

- Understand how to prepare for a listing appointment, and once you understand this, what questions to ask.
- Be able to use dialogues to make a listing presentation.
- Be able to use dialogues for handling questions and objections from sellers.
- Know how to get the listing signed.
- Be able to use dialogues for discussions after you get the listing.

Preparing for the Listing Appointment

Prior to attending a listing appointment, the real estate professional salesperson should prepare by getting basic information about the property from the homeowner and by providing him or her with the essential paperwork and information about the real estate company and the salesperson.

Questions for Getting Information about the Property and Documents

The first step in preparing for the listing appointment is for the real estate professional to talk with the potential client on the telephone. In that initial contact, the salesperson should ask the following questions:

- What is your name?
- What is the exact address of your property?
- What is your home telephone number?
- What is your cell phone number?
- What is your e-mail address?
- Do you prefer to communicate by telephone or by e-mail?
- Is there anyone else who will be helping you make this decision?
- How many square feet are in your home?
- How did you arrive at that number?
- How many bedrooms do you have?
- How many bathrooms do you have?
- How many living areas do you have?
- How many garage spaces do you have?
- Do you have garage door openers?
- Would you describe the kitchen equipment?
- Do you have a fireplace?
- Is the patio outside covered?
- Do you have a wood fence?
- Do you have a security system?
- Do you have a swimming pool or spa?
- Do you have a built-in sprinkler system?
- Does the house need any repairs?

- Are there any extra special features in the house?
- Have you made any major improvements to the property in the last year?
- Why do you want to sell?
- When would you like to make this move?
- What would it do to your plans if you just couldn't sell? How long have you owned this house?
- Are you talking with any other real estate professional at this time?
- If you were going to put your house on the market today, what price would you like to start at?
- How much do you currently owe on the property?
- Do you have any other properties to sell?
- Tell me, why did you buy your current home?
- When you get this house sold, what will you do?
- Where will you be moving to?
- Do you have an agent to help you find a home in that area?
- What are you looking for in a real estate professional that you hire?

These are quite a lot of questions, but you need most of this information in order to do a comparative market analysis.

Before the conversation ends, ask the homeowner to have the essential documents on hand for the listing appointment.

Salesperson: Mr. Vinson, before I come out, could you find your deed, survey, title policy, and any papers you received when you bought the house?

Dialogue about Pre-Listing Packet

A pre-listing packet is a packet of all the paperwork necessary to list the property, a presentation folder, and your real estate resume. You give this packet to the homeowner prior to making the listing presentation. This allows the homeowner the time to read and become familiar with the paperwork. Some homeowners will actually fill the papers out prior to your arrival, saving considerable time.

The presentation folder provides information about your company and includes the marketing plan. Some salespeople have presentation folders that are so good that the homeowner is ready to list as soon as the salesperson walks through the door.

The resume is simply that—your real estate resume. That means it should be only about real estate. If you don't have enough experience in real estate to make up a resume, then leave this out.

Salesperson: Mr. Vinson, I have some information that I would like to deliver to you prior to our appointment on Thursday. I will be bringing this by around six o'clock this evening, if that would be OK. If you're not home, I will leave it at the front door. I'm looking forward to our time together.

If other salespeople are competing for this listing and they do not deliver a pre-listing packet, you will look far more professional.

Here's another professional touch. Prepare a sleeve for a photo, labeling it with the property address and "Presented by (your name)." Then, as you arrive at the address, take an instant photo of the property from your vehicle and place the photo in the sleeve. Digital cameras and computer technology make this effect even better, but if you use a digital camera, you will have to take the picture prior to your visit unless you have a portable photo printer that enables you to turn a digital photo into a print in your car.

Dialogue for Greeting the Seller

When the homeowner answers the door, use the following dialogue:

Salesperson: Mr. Vinson?

Homeowner: Yes?

Salesperson: Dan Hamilton with Acme Realty. We have a meeting at seven o'clock, and (look at your watch) it is now seven o'clock. It is nice to meet you.

You look at your watch to draw attention to the fact that you have arrived on time, that you keep your word.

Next, hand the homeowner the photo of the house with the following words:

Salesperson: Sometimes people do not have pictures of their home, and I thought it would be nice if you had one.

It's a simple but effective way to break the ice. Once you're inside the door, look down at the floor by the door. If you see shoes lined up, you should ask:

Salesperson: Before I go further, would you like me to take off my shoes?

You want to show respect for the homeowners. Some do not like it when people wear shoes in their house. Maybe the homeowners have just installed carpet and don't want dirty shoes walking across it. Now you head to the kitchen, even if the homeowners want to sit in the living room:

Salesperson: Could we sit at the kitchen table?

Homeowner: Wouldn't you be more comfortable in the living room?

Salesperson: Well, I have some material that I would like to show you, and I think it would be better at the kitchen table.

The business decisions in a household are made in the kitchen. Anywhere else puts you at a disadvantage. Now, one last thing:

Salesperson: Before we start, could I get a glass of water?

This simple request allows the homeowners to be hospitable to you and makes them feel friendly. Then you transition into your presentation.

Salesperson: Thanks for the water, and thank you for having me over tonight. Before we get to the presentation, could I show you how I work?

This is not open-heart surgery, but the homeowners may be a little curious about the process. By introducing the presentation, you give the homeowners a chance to relax.

Dialogue for Introducing the Presentation

Salesperson: First of all, we will go over some questions and determine what you want to accomplish by selling this house. Then we will take a look at the property: you tell me what you like and, more important, what you don't like about the house, which will help me market it more effectively. We will then discuss how my company and I are so well qualified to market your property. We will then discuss my personal marketing plan and determine if you like and trust me and if we can work together. Frequently, a real estate agent will tell homeowners what they want to hear just to get the listing. I'd like to speak with you very candidly and tell you the truth about what's needed to get your house sold. May I do that?

Homeowner: Yes.

Making the Presentation

The presentation as structured here consists of nine parts:

- Explaining the concept of agency
- Asking questions of the sellers
- Taking a tour of the property
- Presenting your qualifications
- Presenting the credentials of your company
- Outlining your custom marketing plan
- Discussing pricing
- Getting the signature
- Handling discussions of other matters

Now let's look at dialogues for each of these parts.

Dialogue for Explaining Agency

Salesperson: Generally in real estate, each real estate salesperson will represent either the buyer or the seller. Under the agency law, there are many ways to do this, but we will discuss what I will do for you.

If we agree to work together, I will be representing you. I will help you determine the price you will need to market the house. I will help you on marketing the house. I will discuss the contracts with you and ultimately represent you in every manner possible. Would you want me to represent you?

Homeowner: Yes, we want representation.

Salesperson: At our office, we also work for buyers, representing them in a similar manner as you. We help them find a home, determine a purchase price, and help with contracts. When you decide to buy your next home, would you want representation?

Homeowner: Of course we would.

Salesperson: If a buyer my company is representing wants to buy your house, it will put my broker in what is called an intermediary situation. As an intermediary, the broker would not represent either side. I would remain representing you, and the other agent would remain representing the buyer. Let me ask you this: do you have an objection to your home being shown by an agent representing the buyer?

Homeowner: No, we just want it sold.

Salesperson: Exactly.

This dialogue allows you to cover agency law without a long, tedious discussion. Never ask, "Do you have any questions?" because the homeowner actually might. By asking, "Do you have an objection?" you get permission from the homeowner to move on.

Dialogue for Asking Questions of Sellers

Now you want to ask a series of questions to determine the motivation of the seller. You may have asked some of these questions already, but ask them again. Occasionally homeowners will alter their answers in person from what they told you on the telephone. You should have the questions in writing and show them to the seller. Studies have proved that the salesperson who has a written list of questions is perceived as more organized and professional. Ask the following questions:

1. Why are you moving?
2. When do you want/have to move?
3. How long have you lived in this house?
4. What major improvements have you made in the last year?
5. Whom else are you talking with about the sale of your house?
6. Can you move without selling this house first?
7. Would you consider owner financing?
8. How did you arrive at your price?
9. Do you have any concerns in making a move?
10. What is the most important—price, timing, or convenience?
11. What would it do to your plans if you just couldn't sell?
12. What would it take for you to list with me tonight?

These questions should be asked exactly as written. Each one is essential, and the order for asking them makes a difference. The questions lead the seller through a process of evaluating selling the house, and you have time to decide if you even want the listing. It is always better to walk away from a listing earlier than later. Let's analyze each question:

Why are you moving? This is a simple question, but it gives insight into the homeowner's motivation. If the answer is that the homeowner really does not need to move but would if he or she could get the asking price, that homeowner is not motivated. If the answer is that the homeowner has a job transfer and must be in another state, that homeowner is motivated. We want the homeowner to be motivated, because then he or she will be more realistic about selling. You should already know the answer to this question if you have a listing appointment; nevertheless, you should ask it again. There's a lot of difference between what people tell you over the telephone and what they tell you in person. You can see their eyes and read their body language. This question and the next question are a little tense for the homeowner, because they call for committing to a decision. Expect hesitation.

When do you want/have to move? This is also a simple question, and again it gives insight into the homeowner's motivation. If the answer is that the homeowner can move anytime within the next six years, that homeowner is not motivated. If the answer is that the homeowner must move within the next 60 days, that homeowner is motivated.

How long have you lived in this house? This question is intended to lighten the pressure the homeowner may feel from the first two questions. This question is easy to answer, so he or she does not feel pressure anymore. For you, the value of this question is to enable you to determine the seller's equity position. If the homeowner has purchased the house recently, he or she might not have enough equity in it to pay the closing costs. This would result in the homeowner demanding more for the house than it might be worth.

What major improvements have you made in the last year? The word "major" is important here. Some homeowners seem to believe that if they change a lightbulb, it's an improvement. You must write down all the major improvements they mention, and do not challenge them now. This time is for gathering information and not for discussion. The discussion will come later. This question is meant to determine if there are undisclosed features of the home you need to know that could make a difference in the value of the house. This question causes very little pressure.

Whom else are you talking with about the sale of your house? You want to know if other salespeople are competing for this listing. Know your competitors. Know their strengths and weaknesses. Do not disparage your competitors, but if you offer a service not offered by your competitors, be sure to emphasize that. If the homeowner is not talking with anyone else, that is also good to know. This question could cause a lot of pressure if the homeowner believes he or she is revealing a secret. Some homeowners believe they can play one real estate salesperson against another and receive a better deal. If they disclose this information, they believe it could jeopardize their position.

Can you move without selling this house first? This question is to smoke out any potential problems the homeowner may have, like not enough equity to sell. It also alerts you that the homeowner might be looking at other houses, and you want to be the one to sell him or her that new home. If a homeowner does not need to sell first, ask about the buy side. You don't want to find out later that he or she has bought a home without you.

Would you consider owner financing? Owner financing is when the homeowner helps the buyer with all or part of the financing. If the homeowner is willing to help, it will open up this house to more potential buyers.

How did you arrive at your price? Pricing is usually one of the biggest objections a homeowner will have. Does it surprise anyone that the homeowner wants more than the house is worth? The purpose of this question is to find out how he or she got that price and whether it was based on fact or on need. However, this is not the time to overcome pricing objections.

Do you have any concerns in making a move? Some homeowners may have a reason that will hold them back from moving. It would be very disappointing if you worked hard on selling a property and you received a good offer, and then the homeowner declined the offer because the family did not want to sell before the end of the school year or their new home would not be ready for another three months.

What is the most important—price, timing, or convenience? These are the big three factors that motivate homeowners.

So which factor is more important to your potential clients: the money, the length of time it takes to sell, or the convenience of selling and moving on with their lives?

What would it do to your plans if you just couldn't sell? Some homeowners don't believe they have to sell. This question makes them think ahead and maybe become a little more reasonable.

What would it take for you to list with me tonight? This is the most important question to ask; you must ask it every time. This question is a little intimidating to the real estate salesperson because it feels like exerting high pressure. Don't mellow the question: ask it as written. The reason this question is so important is because you are asking for any final objections, and you are asking it up front. It is easier to ask it now because it is not threatening to the seller at this point. If you wait until you begin to close, the homeowner might clam up. Also, asking it now allows you plenty of time to overcome any objections.

Dialogue for Taking a Tour of the Property

Once you are finished asking your questions, you will want to tour the property, including outdoors. Your conversion dialogue would be this:

Salesperson: Great! Now, could you show me through the house?

Let the owner walk you through the house. As always, you write down anything the owner says. Yes, even if it's boring stuff like "This is the bathroom." You might comment, "OK, let me take a look."

Do not mention anything good about the house. Quite the contrary, you should gently point out flaws. Never say, "Wow, what a beautiful room! You must love the time spent in here." If you say such positive things, you can count on the price being jacked up. However, if you notice a spot on the carpet, for example, you should comment.

Salesperson: What about that?
Homeowner: We had a spill.
Salesperson: Will you replace the carpet?
Homeowner: Is that necessary, or should we try to have the carpets cleaned first?
Salesperson: Well, that sounds like a good idea. When will you be able to have them cleaned professionally?

This tour dialogue is to show the homeowner the reality of the house: it's not the mansion the owner may have imagined. You never say, "Do this or that." If you suggest something like "You should replace the carpets," the owner will feel betrayed if the property does not sell. If you ask the correct questions, as demonstrated here, you can lead the homeowner to draw the right conclusions. Here's an example:

Homeowner: We had a spill. Should we have the carpets cleaned?

Salesperson: I would.

Do you see how this is much nicer and noncommittal?

Do not forget: this is the time to build rapport. Ask why the owner bought the house. If you see golf clubs or an interesting picture, ask about it.

Salesperson: Wow, what a great picture of skiing! Are you big on that?

The homeowner now can talk about things unrelated to the house, giving him or her time to like you and trust you and build that necessary rapport.

Once the tour is over, head back to the kitchen table to continue your presentation with the homeowners.

Salesperson: OK, is there anything else you would like to tell me about the property?

Homeowner: No, I don't think so.

Salesperson: All right. Then let me tell you a little about myself and how I can help you sell your property.

Dialogue for Presenting Your Qualifications

During this section of the listing presentation, you should discuss your personal ability to sell the house. If you don't have a lot of experience, then you should leave out this section.

Salesperson: I would first like to share with you my commitment. I am not here just to list your home. I am looking to establish a long-term relationship with you. I promise to meet or exceed all your expectations in getting your property sold so that I earn the right to get all your future business and referrals to your friends, relatives, and business associates. Your input is critical to my success. If I do a great job marketing and selling your home, would you be willing to write a letter of recommendation for me?

Homeowner: Sure.

The best time to ask for a recommendation letter is prior to the listing. If you wait till closing to ask, the occasion may not arise, and you'll miss out on a chance to build your business.

Salesperson: My responsibility is to get buyers through the property. I will provide you honest feedback on the condition of your property. I will provide you data and experience to price your home competitively. I will communicate feedback from other sales associates and potential buyers and follow up administratively on the contract of sale.

This dialogue tells the homeowner that you will personally handle all aspects of the transaction. Then you go on to discuss your education, awards, honors, recognitions, years in the business (if over five years), and real estate production statistics, along with a list of satisfied customers.

Dialogue for Closing Presentation of Qualifications

The biggest mistake a real estate salesperson typically makes is not to close each section prior to moving to the next section. If you do not close this section, the homeowner may not know how or when to ask any additional questions. Then at the end, you get hit with a ton of questions and objections, and you panic and lose the opportunity to list the property. If you close now and the homeowner is not satisfied with your presentation, he or she will let you know. It is better to handle any problem now than to wait and let the problem arise at the end.

Salesperson: Do you have any questions about what I personally can do to help you sell your home?

Homeowner: No, I think you've covered it.

Salesperson: After seeing the things I have to offer, do you believe I can sell your house for you?

Homeowner: Yes, you sound very capable.

Salesperson: Great! Now let's look at what my company can do for you.

This last line makes a transition to the next section. But if the homeowner does not give you a definite affirmative answer, you must probe further:

Salesperson: After seeing the things I have to offer, do you believe I can sell your house for you?

Homeowner: I guess.

Salesperson: Whoa! That did not sound convincing. I must know that you believe in me before I can proceed. Do you believe that I can get your house sold, or is there something that is not clear or needs further discussion?

Homeowner: No, no, I believe you can sell this home.

By expecting a definite affirmative answer, you make the homeowner either commit to believing that you can sell the house or come out with any objections. Either way you win.

Sometimes it takes the tough questions from the salesperson to get the listing. We may think that it would be too abrasive to say that, but the opposite is actually true.

Homeowners want a representative who is strong and confident as the person to sell their most valuable possession. If you're thinking that such a salesperson would make you mad talking that way, my response to you or the client would be, "You don't really want to sell your home, do you?" Because if you did, you would want the best advocate for your position you could find. Suppose you are on trial for a serious crime and could spend the rest of your life behind bars. You know you're innocent. Do you want a wimp for an attorney? I don't think so! There is no difference in the eyes of the homeowner.

Salesperson: Great! Now let's look at what my company can do for you.

Dialogue for Discussing Your Company

If you're an agent with few real estate accomplishments, this section should be the most in-depth. Spend a great deal of time explaining what your company can do to help the homeowner sell by presenting:

- Your company history
- Your company statistics
- Your company awards and recognitions
- Addresses of properties that your company has sold
- A list of satisfied clients of your company

You may have to work through your broker or an administrative assistant to get some of these facts. Remember: you are a member of your company, so that makes each sale our sale. When you have the facts, use the following dialogue.

Salesperson: Mr. and Mrs. Vinson, here's a list of addresses of some properties we've sold in the past year. With this vast list of homes we have sold, you can be sure that we can sell yours!

Dialogue for Closing the Company Section

Once you have completed the company section of the listing presentation, you should close that section. The following is a dialogue you could use.

Salesperson: Do you have any questions about what my company can do to help you sell your home?

Homeowner: No.

Salesperson: After seeing the things my company has to offer, do you believe that we can sell your house for you?

Homeowner: Yes.

Salesperson: Great! Now let's look at what my custom marketing plan can do for you.

Dialogue for Presenting Your Custom Marketing Plan

In this section you should cover your custom marketing plan with the homeowners. You design the custom marketing plan for their specific situation. This sounds a whole lot more complicated than it actually is. There are certain things you do each and every time to sell a listing, such as putting up a For Sale sign, putting up a key box, placing the listing in the Multiple Listing Service, running advertisements, and distributing flyers. Just assign specific dates to each of those things. You have now created a custom marketing plan. Most real-estate-specific client management software systems will do this for you. The following provides examples of some items you can use; the number of items is only limited by you.

Salesperson: Mr. and Mrs. Vinson, do you know about the Multiple Listing Service?

Homeowner: A little bit.

Salesperson: Well, the Multiple Listing Service, the MLS, is a database of all available properties in a given area. The MLS provides exposure to the greatest number of potential buyers, because every real estate professional will know your property is available for sale. Over 70 percent of residential sales involve the MLS system in some way. The MLS provides additional security, because all salespersons are licensed by the state, and it provides the best access to potential relocation buyers. Mr. and Mrs. Vinson, can you see the advantages of participating in the MLS?

Homeowner: Yes.

Salesperson: Mr. and Mrs. Vinson, did you know that advertising generates only about 2 percent of sales on the specific residential properties advertised?

Homeowner: No. I thought it was more than that.

Salesperson: Then why do you think we still advertise if the specific success rate is that low?

Homeowner: I don't know.

Salesperson: Because what advertising does is it identifies buyers in general. Suppose we advertise a house down the street from you. A buyer calls us about it, I describe it, and the caller quickly realizes that he won't like that particular house. But he likes the area. So I can then guide that buyer to your house. Do you see the process?

Homeowner: That makes sense.

Salesperson: Would you like the real estate company that you hire to advertise regularly?

Homeowner: Of course.

Salesperson: Let's look at what my company does to get your house sold through advertising.

Homeowner: OK.

Salesperson: We currently advertise in the local newspaper in the real estate section. We advertise in the real estate magazine that is distributed across the city, and we advertise in the relocation magazine that is given to relocation specialists across the nation. Do you feel that we have covered all the bases on print advertising?

Homeowner: Well, yes, it seems like it.

Salesperson: Mr. and Mrs. Vinson, could you guess what the current, most frequent way is that a buyer looks for a home?

Homeowner: I would assume the Internet, 'cause that is what I would do.

Salesperson: Precisely! Would you require your next real estate company to have complete coverage of the Internet before you would hire them?

Homeowner: Yes, I would.

Salesperson: We at Acme Realty agree. We have access to many Web sites and search engines that drive potential buyers to our company. We are part of the RealEstate.com Web site, the LocalRealEstate.com Web site, and the ResidentialRealEstate.com Web site. All these sites create interest in your property. Would you like me to get your property exposed on these Web sites today?

The previous dialogues have covered many things, but the main thing you should notice is the dialogue structure. Start with a question, then proceed with a description, and finalize with another question. If you can do that, you can construct dialogues using your specific marketing items.

Dialogue for Closing the the Custom Marketing Plan Section

As always, you should close this section before moving on to the next section.

Salesperson: So do you have any questions about my custom marketing plan and what it can do to help you sell your home?

Homeowner: No.

Salesperson: After seeing the things that my custom marketing plan has to offer, do you believe it will sell your house for you?

Homeowner: Yes.

Salesperson: Great! Now let's look at pricing the house for sale.

Dialogue for Pricing—General

The pricing section could be the most important. It is covered last because we are setting up the idea that we are the experts and can sell houses. If the homeowner does not believe we can sell his or her house, then pricing does not even matter, because we will not get the listing.

The temptation is to bring out the comparative market analysis (CMA) and hammer the homeowner with market facts. But the CMA is a tool, not a weapon. We should not beat the homeowners with it. As a matter of fact, I rarely cover it prior to reaching an agreement with the owner on price.

To get the homeowner to price the property correctly, you should ask a lot of clarifying questions. You may have asked some of these questions on the telephone prior to the listing appointment, but ask them again.

Salesperson: If you were going to put the house on the market, what would you want to price it at?

Salesperson: How did you arrive at that price?

Salesperson: What would it do to your plans if you couldn't sell?

The purpose of clarifying questions is to get the homeowner to see the reality of the situation. If you deal with his or her emotions and listen for clues to what's motivating him or her, obtaining the correct price will be natural. Here are some additional dialogues you can use.

Dialogues on Pricing

DIALOGUE ON PRICING I

Salesperson: There are five reasons a property sells—location, price, terms, condition of the property, and real estate professional representing the property. The good news is that you control all these except the location of your house.

DIALOGUE ON PRICING II

Salesperson: What you paid for your house doesn't affect its value. The amount of cash you need from your house to buy your new home doesn't affect its value. What you want for your house doesn't affect its value. What any real estate salesperson says your house is worth doesn't affect its value. Mr. and Mrs. Vinson, do you know the only thing that affects the value of your house?

Homeowner: No.

Salesperson: The value of your house is determined by what a buyer is willing to pay in today's market based on comparing your house with others currently on the market for sale. Buyers always determine value.

DIALOGUE ON PRICING III

Salesperson: When it comes to pricing your house, we should remember that buyers are more likely to view houses that are priced right. Your price should be based on sold comparables, properties similar to yours in this area, rather than on properties that are still on the market. Properties that are priced high help sell houses that are priced right. Overpriced properties take longer to sell and usually end up selling below market price. Many agents suggest a high price to the homeowners just to get the listing. But we cannot work miracles. Buyers always determine value. Based on what has sold in the immediate area, it looks like your house should be priced at $285,000. Considering all this information, at what price would you like to offer your home for sale?

DIALOGUE ON PRICING IV

Salesperson: Mr. and Mrs. Vinson, now that you have seen these comparable house prices, it appears your home should sell for $280,000. Will you list your home for that price tonight?

Homeowner: We just can't do that. We need more money. We can't take a dime less than $300,000.

Salesperson: There are some important questions I would like to ask you. Why do you feel your home is worth $10,000 to $20,000 more than your neighbor's?

Homeowner: Well, we did a lot of repairs on this house when we bought it.

Salesperson: What did you pay for it, may I ask?

Homeowner: $250,000.

Salesperson: Are you telling me you spent $50,000 fixing this place up?

Homeowner: Well, maybe not that much, but it was a lot.

Salesperson: How much do you think you spent?

Homeowner: Easily $20,000 to $25,000.

Salesperson: Well, you paid $250,000 and put $25,000 into it. That would make it $275,000, right around the price we were talking. Could we go ahead and put your property on the market tonight for $280,000?

Homeowner: That still does not get us what we want.

Salesperson: If you were looking to purchase a home in this area and two were for sale, one for $280,000 and another one for $300,000, and both were virtually the same quality and had the same amenities, which would you buy?

Homeowner: Not all houses are the same.

Salesperson: To this buyer, you, let's assume they seem the same. Which would you buy, the one for $280,000 or the one for $300,000?

Homeowner: Well, sure, you would buy the cheaper one.

Salesperson: Don't you feel most people will feel just like you? Mr. and Mrs. Vinson, I know this is not what you wanted, but don't you see the value in pricing your property correctly? Could we start today at $280,000 and get you happily moved?

Be prepared for long dialogues when it comes time for pricing. It is the main drawback for homeowners. If you want more on how to handle the pricing objection, be sure you read the Chapter 8 of this book.

DIALOGUE FOR CLOSING THE PRICING SECTION

You must close this section or run the risk that the owner will later catch you by surprise.

Salesperson: Don't you agree that we should market your property at $280,000?

Dialogue for the Final Close

Final close sounds so serious, but if you have presented your material correctly and closed each section, the final close is actually easy:

Salesperson: Put me to work for you!

That dialogue is simple and to the point. There's no fancy stuff here. It's time to ask for the commitment.

Fill in the paperwork, and then leave. Don't hang around. Remember to get a set of keys and the security code. Be sure and measure the rooms. Then get the listing signed.

Salesperson: All we need to do now is simply sign this listing agreement so I can get you what you want in the time you want it. Won't that be great?

or:

Salesperson: All we need to do now is simply decide to use my service so I can help you get what you want in the time you want it. Won't that be great?

Dialogues for Post-Signing Discussions

A post-signing discussion is when the real estate professional discusses with the homeowner some marketing issues that are best discussed after the homeowner has agreed to list. These are typically sensitive subjects, and you do not want to upset a homeowner before you get that signature. The next dialogues give guidance on these discussions.

DIALOGUE ON ADVERTISING

Advertising is usually done on a rotation basis, which means that a house may be advertised only once per month or less. Some homeowners believe this is not acceptable; they want their house advertised every day in every publication.

Salesperson: Mr. and Mrs. Vinson, here is a newspaper showing some houses for sale. Your house is being advertised with them. Can you find it?

Homeowner (after a moment of looking): It's not there.

Salesperson: Yes, it is. Would you like to know what I mean?

Homeowner: Yes.

Salesperson: You see, a buyer will call our office about a house in this ad, and it will not work out for them. After asking some questions about what the buyer wants, we feel that your home may be of interest, so we show it—and we sell it. So even if your home is not "pictured" every week, it is being advertised constantly. Does that make sense?

DIALOGUE ON DEALING WITH UNSCHEDULED VISITS

Part of our duty is to protect our seller clients. It is difficult to say, "Be careful!" because we don't want to alarm them and cause them to think that selling their houses will be dangerous. So we will approach this matter with the following dialogue.

Salesperson: Mr. and Mrs. Vinson, if any people show up at your door wanting to see the house or show the house without having arranged an appointment with us, please do not let them into the house. Give them one of my cards, and tell them to call me. We need to track all the people who go through the house so we can get feedback on how they felt about the property, and we cannot do that if we have no record. It should never happen, but just in case, send them away; they should know better. Will you do this for me?

DIALOGUE ABOUT NOT SIGNING ANY PAPERS

Rarely does it happen that homeowners sign papers without their representative, but if it happened, it could be bad. If homeowners sign a document because they think it's necessary and thus obligate themselves to something without consulting their representative, lawsuits could result. As their representative, you should always know what is going on.

Salesperson: If at any time someone, such as a title officer, wants you to sign something that I have not approved, don't do it until I see it. I want to be sure that everything is correct before your signature goes on it. Can we agree to that?

DIALOGUE TO PREPARE THE HOMEOWNER FOR A QUICK OFFER

This is a great thing and also a dangerous thing. You list the property and then receive a full-price offer the next day. It's great because you've sold the property. It's dangerous because the seller may think that the house was under-priced. If it seems like he or she has left money on the table, the seller will always blame the real estate professional, when in reality the seller just got lucky in finding a buyer that quickly.

Salesperson: Mr. and Mrs. Vinson, if we get a full-price offer tomorrow, let's feel we got lucky and not that the house is underpriced. There are buyers out in the market right now; when your house hits the market, they will come see it. If it's what they want, they will pay you market price. If we don't recognize that, we could lose them, and it could take months to find another buyer. Does what I am saying make sense to you?

DIALOGUE FOR ARRANGING A CREATIVE OPEN HOUSE

Open houses can be a great way to generate buyer interest for a specific property. But what happens if the house you are listing is not conducive to having an open house? Suppose it is in a hidden area at a long distance from the main traffic areas. Here's a dialogue for handling that situation.

Salesperson: We will hold an open house on your property, Mr. and Mrs. Vinson, just not here at the house. Do you know what I mean by that?'

Homeowner: Uh, no.

Salesperson: Your house is the house buyers want. It is located in a secluded area away from the hassle of the city. But that location is a problem for holding an open house here, because most drive-by buyers will get lost getting here. What we will do is hold an open house on a property that is located on a main road. Potential buyers will stop because it is on their way somewhere. They will love the house, but hate the location. So then we bring those buyers here. So you see, your house will be held open, just not here. Now, aren't you glad your house is away from heavy traffic?

DIALOGUE ABOUT SHOWING THE PROPERTY

There are several things that homeowners should know about having their house on the market and being shown.

Salesperson: Now that your house is on the market, you should be aware of a few things.

First, I will not show it as much as other agents will. That is good. My job is to get your home sold, not to sell it. I will be marketing to all the other agents in the area and to their buyers. This will generate a lot more traffic through your house than only me alone. The more legitimate buyers through the property, the more money you will obtain in a shorter time.

Second, our company sets all the appointments, so someone will call you about every showing scheduled. Please be tolerant of the occasional showing by a buyer's agent who is parked out front. Their buyers may have just wanted to see this house; if it's what they want, we've just made a sale. So please do not refuse any showings.

Third, it is best if you leave during showings. It allows the buyer to feel more comfortable and less distracted. So could I ask you to leave for a short time during showings?

Homeowner: Yes, we can do that.

Salesperson: I hate to do this to you, but the house must remain in show condition at all times. You may not have time to prepare for each showing, and we want every potential buyer to see your house in the best light. So could we have everything picked up and the house ready to show at all times?

Homeowner: Sure, we understand—keep the house clean at all times.

Salesperson: Great! Thanks. That helps me help you. One last thing on showings. . . . If we don't get any showings or very few showings within the first month, it would mean that buyers are rejecting the price, and no amount of marketing will change that. I will then ask you to adjust your price. The opposite would be true if we get a lot of showings but no offers. If that happens, it would indicate that the buyers are rejecting something specifically about the house. I would then determine what it is and see if we can do something together to correct the problem. Does all that make sense to you two?

DIALOGUE ON BEING AWAY FROM HOME

If the homeowner leaves the property for more than a day at a time, you must know, because it is important to be able to contact him or her if an offer comes in.

Salesperson: If you ever leave for an extended period of time, even a day or two, be sure to let me know. You never know when I might need to get hold of you. As long as I can reach you, you can go anywhere at any time. So I have your cell number, but will you still call me before you leave town?

DIALOGUE ON KEEPING IN CONTACT

To help with your time management, set a time for calling the homeowners. Otherwise, they will call you at every whim, and you will get no work done—especially if you have 30 or 40 listings! And if you promise to call them, you'd better call them.

Salesperson: I will be calling you every Monday at six o'clock in the evening. I will update you on showings, inquiries, and any other activity that has occurred on the property. If you have any questions in the meantime, please write them down, and we will discuss them at that time. Will you do that for me?

DIALOGUE ON A PRICE REDUCTION AGREEMENT

It may be good to initiate a price reduction schedule from the beginning. This way the homeowner expects it, and it is not as big a deal.

Salesperson: Mr. and Mrs. Vinson, each month you will get a price reduction agreement from me by e-mail. This letter is automatically set from today for 30 days out. Don't be alarmed when you get it. You can do any of three things with it. First, you can delete it. If the number of showings is what you think it should be, then by all means delete it. The second thing you can do is to print it off, put the price adjustment in the blank, sign it, and mail it back to me. I do need this by mail, according to our rules. One thing, though: you should adjust it by at least 5 percent. Any less and buyers don't notice it, so it does us no good. We then can market the reduction and attract other potential buyers. The third thing you can do is to put it in your saved file and think about it. If after a couple of days you think you may want to adjust the price, then you still have it. Does all that seem fair to you, Mr. and Mrs. Vinson?

DIALOGUE TO CROSS-SELL OTHER COMPANY SERVICES

If your company offers other services, this is when you would close to get those sold. Your company could own a mortgage company, be affiliated with a home warranty company, or offer any number of ancillary services.

Salesperson: That should cover it. Oh, by the way, let me show you this. Here is a list of the people with whom we work directly. Those are our preferred vendors; they give our clients the best services at the best prices. I suggest you look at that list and use those vendors as often as you can. I know you mentioned you needed to get some electrical work done; there are three professionals on this list who can take care of that for you. Would you like for me to have one of them call you?

Chapter 7
Dialogues for Working with Buyers

Buyers are considered easy money in the real estate business. All you have to do is show properties, and eventually the client will buy and you will make money. In reality, this is the hard way to work.

The real estate professional should have a system for handling the buyer during the purchase process. This chapter is intended to teach the salesperson the correct way to work with a buyer for everyone's benefit.

This chapter presents and discusses the following:

- Dialogues for the presentation
- Dialogues for handling objections from buyers
- Dialogues for showing a property
- Dialogues for writing an offer

This chapter is intended for practically anyone in the real estate industry, including salespeople, brokers, and managers. It is specifically of benefit to salespeople who specialize in buyer representation.

Dialogues for Working with Buyers

These are the objectives of this chapter:

- Understand the process of working with a buyer.
- Be able to list and use questions to help the buyer make the correct decisions.
- Be able to design a buyer presentation and use the dialogues given.
- Be able to handle the buyer's objections.

Dialogue for Meeting with Buyers

The professional real estate salesperson should meet any potential buyer in the real estate office conference room. The meeting is a qualifying meeting. The following dialogues and questions should be used.

Salesperson: Thank you for meeting me here. It would be very helpful to me if I knew something about you, your family, and your ultimate objectives. The better I understand your reasons for buying a home, the easier it will make finding the right home for you. Does that make sense?

Buyer: Sure.

Salesperson: Great! I'd like to begin by asking you a couple of questions. May I do that?

BUYER PRESENTATION MANUAL

You should develop a buyer presentation manual to use with potential buyers, and you should bring it out right after you have the preceding dialogue. The manual is a visual aid for your presentation. The following dialogues assume you have a buyer presentation manual and are using it.

To put a manual together, simply put into print form the items you are going to discuss, and place them in a binder. You should include:

- Information on agency law
- Questions for the wants-and-needs analysis
- Information on how you work
- Information on personal results
- Information on company results
- An activity plan

Dialogue for Discussing Agency Law

You should begin the presentation by discussing agency law with your potential clients. Proper agency disclosure concerning your legal obligations to both the buyers and the sellers may be required by state laws or local regulations. This discussion should be short and not too detailed—more of a summary.

Salesperson: First of all, do you understand about agency law?

Buyer: I'm not sure.

Salesperson: Agency law regulates the real estate industry and whom we represent during the transaction. I will be representing you two during this entire process, if you agree.

Buyer: Sure.

If you need more discussion according to your real estate commission, you may need to extend this dialogue. Be careful, though: too much talk on laws and regulations that is not required could end up scaring the clients. We must make sure our clients are aware of things that are important. But ultimately, our job is to protect them, not scare them.

Questions for Doing a
Wants-and-Needs Analysis

You should continue the presentation by asking a number of qualifying questions. This is the start of a wants-and-needs analysis. A wants-and-needs analysis helps identify a potential client's buying or selling wants and needs. Wants are desires; needs are requirements. The analysis helps you to match buyers' and sellers' wants, needs, and motives with the specific properties available.

The wants-and-needs analysis will give you an opportunity to read your clients better and fully understand their wants and needs. Any property shown must meet all their needs, but it can satisfy any or none of the wants. Any want a property satisfies is a bonus. If no properties meet all their needs, you must narrow their requirements through the use of questioning dialogues. Remember, though, that the decision to buy a particular house is often more emotional than practical and that the wants-and-needs analysis is an expression of the buyer's logical thoughts. Don't be disappointed or surprised if the buyer chooses a house that is completely different than the analysis describes. You should ask questions like the following:

1. Why are you wanting to buy?
2. When do you want/have to move?
3. Do you own, or are you currently renting?
4. How long have you lived at your present residence?
5. Who else are you talking with about purchasing a house?
6. Have you spoken with a mortgage company?
7. What price range were you considering?

8. What is the maximum monthly payment that you would be comfortable with?

9. Do you have any concerns in making a move?

10. Which is the most important factor—price, timing, or convenience?

11. What would it do to your plans if you just couldn't buy?

12. What would it take for you to agree to work with me today?

These questions should be asked at any buyer presentation. These are considered the basic buyer questions. You could also ask the following additional questions:

- How many bedrooms do you need?
- How will you use the third bedroom? Will it be a guest room or an office?
- Is a dining room important? Why?
- Are there any special features you must have in your home?
- What do you want in a home? What features?
- If there were no other way, where could you be flexible? What feature could you do without?
- Will anyone else be living in your new home?
- Are you familiar with today's procedures for buying a home?
- Have you seen any homes that you liked?
- Have you made any written offers?
- What do you like best about your present home?
- What do you like least about your present home?
- In which area do you prefer to live?
- What are your requirements for your next home?

- Where do you work?
- Would you prefer a large down payment and smaller monthly payments or a small down payment and larger monthly payments?
- If we found the right home but you needed a few thousand dollars more, could you come up with it?
- If we found the perfect home but it was a couple of dollars a day more, could you find the extra money?
- If I could arrange for the lender to take your application today, would you be available?
- What do you like to do in your spare time?
- What are your hobbies?
- Where are you from originally?
- What type of business are you in?
- What three main things do you want in your new home?
- How much time do you want to spend driving to and from work?
- Are you a veteran?
- How many people are in your family?
- Do you want the right to inspect the home before you close?
- Are you going to use an attorney or title company?
- Do you have an insurance policy that you can withdraw funds from for your down payment?
- Will your employer be willing to pay any of your closing costs?
- If we found the perfect home today, would you be willing to buy it?

If you take your clients on more than three to five showing

appointments and still have no strong possibilities, perhaps you should sit down and reevaluate their wants and needs. Wrap up the wants-and-needs analysis section of your buyer presentation with the following dialogue:

Salesperson: I really appreciate your answering these questions. I think I now understand more about you two and your objectives. Now I would like to discuss a little about how we will work together in this homebuying process.

Dialogue for Explaining How You Work

Buying a house is not rocket science, but it can be a little scary. The "How I Work" section of your presentation will reassure the buyer that you have a set plan for helping him or her find and buy a home.

Salesperson: Mr. and Mrs. Vinson, my job is to work as hard as I can to find you the home that meets all your needs and has at least a few of those things that you really want. You and your family must feel completely good about the home. But I can't do that without your help. So I will do three things for you if you will do three things for me. Does that seem fair?

Buyer: Depends on the things.

Salesperson: True. The first thing I will do for you is to give you all my expertise and service in the real estate business. This expertise will help us locate your house, because I know where to find the best values. I will continue to search until we have located that special property just for you. Is that of value to you?

Buyer: Yes, it is.

Salesperson: I was hoping you would agree with that. The second thing I will do for you is to use all the technology available to analyze your prospective home. We will be able to determine the value as well as the condition. We don't want to make any mistakes when it comes time to make an offer. Would you want to overpay for your next home?

Buyer: Of course not.

Salesperson: Agreed. Let's get the best value we can. The third thing I will do for you is to use my time and resources to help you in your search. Understand that finding you a home will cost me hard-dollar cash. I will pay for gasoline, cell charges, real estate fees, Multiple Listing Service dues, commission fees, office supplies, office expenses, and many other items that add up that I will have to absorb. And of course, I will use my most precious asset—my time. Do you want me to help you in this manner?

Buyer: Yes.

Salesperson: Good. Now here's what you can do for me. First, if your situation changes, you'll let me know as soon as possible so I will not continue searching for a home for you. Also, if you ever feel unsatisfied with my performance, you will notify me immediately. Is that fair?

Buyer: Of course.

Salesperson: Second, if you see any home and I am not with you, you will give me the opportunity to provide you with information about it. You see, I can help you with any property as long as you let me. If you see an open house, a new build, or a For Sale By Owner property without me, I can't get involved and protect you. Does that make sense?

Buyer: Yes.

Salesperson: The third is that, as long as you believe that I'm giving you the best professional help and working in your best interest, you will work only with me until I find the right home for you. The way we can do that is through a buyer representation agreement. Will you consider putting our relationship in writing?

Buyer: We would consider that.

Salesperson: Great! Now let me tell you a little about what I can do to help you through the process of buying your next home.

Dialogue for Presenting Personal Results

This section is to describe the things you will personally do to help your client find and purchase a home. This section should show the value in you. The following would be some of what your presentation could cover:

- Any real estate education and real estate seminars
- Any real estate awards, recognitions, certifications, and designations you have received
- Years in the real estate business (if over five years)
- Any real estate articles and news stories that have featured you
- Any real estate investments in which you have been involved
- Results statistics
- Names of streets on which you have sold properties
- List of satisfied customers

Salesperson: I can assure you that I have the ability to help you find a home. I have taken all the necessary real estate training in finding potential properties, valuing property, negotiating, and closing transactions. During the last 10 years, I have earned the honor of top producer and have helped an average of 22 families per year get happily moved.

If you have no real estate accomplishments, then eliminate this section and concentrate on the next, talking about your company. As your career develops, begin backing off your company accomplishments and concentrate more on your personal accomplishments. People buy the real estate agent, so you must sell yourself!

Dialogue for Closing the Personal Section

The biggest mistake a real estate salesperson typically makes is not to close each section prior to moving to the next section. If you do not close, the buyer may have additional questions that he or she does not know to ask at this time. It is better to handle them now than to wait and let problems arise at the end.

Salesperson: Any questions about what I personally can do in the purchase process?

Buyer: No, I think you've covered it.

Salesperson: After seeing the things I have to offer, do you believe I can find you your next home?

Buyer: Yes, you sound very capable.

Salesperson: Great! Now let's look at what my company can do for you.

Now that you have closed this section, move on to discussing your company.

Dialogue for Presenting Company Results

For newer agents and those with few real estate accomplishments, the company section should be the most in-depth. Spend a lot of time explaining what your company can do to help the buyer, including:

- Company history, awards, and recognition
- Company statistics on production
- Addresses of properties that your company has sold
- List of satisfied clients of your company

Salesperson: My company has been in business for over 30 years. A company that has been around that long must be taking care of business, don't you agree?

Buyer: Yes.

Salesperson: During that time we have successfully helped over five thousand families get happily moved. We have been awarded the top honor at numerous regional award rallies. We continue to provide quality service to our clients. Do you want to do business with a company that has a proven track record?

Buyer: Of course.

You may have to work through your broker to get some of these facts. Remember: you are a member of your company, and that makes each sale our sale. This dialogue is short and to the point. Clients will react differently to each area of information. If a buyer indicates an interest in more, give more. The dialogue can be extended easily by including more of the items listed above. You will want to close this section to be sure you have covered enough.

Dialogue for Closing the Company Section

Just as for the preceding section, you must close this section to avoid having objections arise about your company later. Here is your dialogue:

Salesperson: Mr. and Mrs. Vinson, with all that my company can offer you, do you believe that we can find you a home that you will be thrilled to call your own?

Buyer: Yes, I believe you can.

Salesperson: All right. Now let's discuss a specific activity plan to discover the home of your dreams.

Again, don't miss the importance of closing each section. You will find out quickly if you have or have not completed this section to the satisfaction of your clients.

Dialogue for Discussing the Activity Plan

The activity plan section is very specific on the details it will take to get the buyer into a home. This comprehensive section should be in bullet form and include virtually everything it takes from now until after closing. You should discuss your value package and how those things in the value package can help the buyer. You should include at least the following activities in assisting the buyers to find their new home:

- Use the Multiple Listing Service to find potential properties for you.
- Check the Internet for additional sources of potential properties for you.
- Attend open houses to learn if any meet your criteria.
- Attend local Board of Realtors® meeting to find out about properties just listed on the market.
- Collect color photos of each house with descriptions for review later.
- Direct-mail, fax, e-mail, or hand-deliver information to area residents inquiring about interest in selling their homes to you.
- Direct-mail, fax, e-mail, or hand-deliver information to For Sale By Owners inquiring about interest in selling their homes to you.
- Direct-mail, fax, e-mail, or hand-deliver information to cooperating real estate offices to probe for potential new listings.
- Present your criteria at real estate office meeting for input from salespeople and their current sellers.

- Tour each home with the eyes of an appraiser, an inspector, a lender, and a buyer.
- Provide necessary contracts for property purchase.
- Help you make a buying decision.
- Request a home warranty plan to protect the home you are considering.
- Engage in contract negotiation when we submit an offer on a home.
- Provide real estate advice throughout the process.
- Provide a broker price opinion and competitive market analysis to determine if the asking price is in line with the market.
- Create buyer's cost sheet to determine estimated costs of sale.
- Follow up on removal of contingencies.
- Work with you and the lender to obtain a loan.
- Work with other agent to set the home up for title work.
- Shake your hand at closing and hand you the keys.

These are but a few of the activities that could be in your value package. Each one could be used as a closing dialogue. To find out how, refer to the book *Real Estate Marketing and Sales Essentials: Steps for Success* by Dan Hamilton.

Salesperson: Mr. and Mrs. Vinson, my list of activities is a detailed plan to set in motion events that will help you find your next home and culminate in a closed transaction. Each of these activities may only generate one extra potential property, but if it helps us locate that special property for you, would you want me to make that effort?

Buyer: Well, yeah.

Dialogue for Closing the Activity Plan Section

You should close this section with the following dialogue:

Salesperson: So do you believe my activity plan can help you get into your next home in the shortest period of time and with the least money out of your pocket?

Buyer: Wow, you will do all that to help us find a home?!

Salesperson: Yes, because I care about you. Do you have any questions about the activity plan?

Buyer: No, it looks like you have it down.

Salesperson: Thank you. Now let's talk about the most crucial aspect of owning a home—and that is me working for you.

Dialogue for the Final Close

The final close is asking for the commitment. This is when you ask the client to sign a buyer representation agreement to work exclusively with you. The final close should be a natural process if you have completed the buyer presentation correctly. Here is an example of the final close dialogue:

Salesperson: Do you see how having me work for you will help you find the best home for you at the best price in the shortest amount of time?

Buyer: Yes.

Salesperson: Great! All we have to do is put together some paperwork, and we will find you your home!

It's not complicated or tricky, because you closed each section earlier. At this point you fill in the buyer representation agreement and get the clients to sign it. You then get them pre-qualified through your mortgage officer. Once the mortgage officer tells you the amount for which the buyers are qualified, you begin your search for potential properties. You then set the showings and show the properties.

Questions to Ask Inside the Property

When you and your client are inside a property you're showing, use the following questions.

- I could see you living here, couldn't you?
- Whose room would this be?
- Would you like to take a quick look back through before we leave?
- Would you buy this house at any price?
- If I could get you into this house for $5,000 less, would you even consider it?
- What did you like best about this house?
- Would you consider this house as your next home?
- Why did you like the second house more than the first?
- You mentioned that you'd like a large backyard. Would you tell me more about how you'd use that yard?
- Would your furniture fit in here OK?
- Is this location suitable for your family?
- How do you feel about the work that needs to be done?
- Would this be the children's bedroom or the guest room?
- If you decide on this one, what will you change about it?

Dialogues for Closing the Sale

Once you find a property that interests your clients, you must close them for the sale. If you fail to do this, your clients will not get their home, and you will not get any income. Buyers are hesitant to commit. You must help them: it is what they want and what you are paid to get them to do. If you're just taking orders, get a job at a burger joint!

DIALOGUE FOR A DIRECT CLOSE

Salesperson: Mr. and Mrs. Vinson, do you want to buy this house?

You would use the direct close when you know the clients love the house and it is perfect for them. You also can tell that they are not hesitant.

DIALOGUE FOR AN ASSUMPTIVE CLOSE

The assumptive close would be used when the clients want the house but are a little scared and may balk at the direct close.

Salesperson: Mr. and Mrs. Vinson, let's see how this looks on paper. Please understand that this does not obligate you in any way. It will help us see how the whole thing looks in writing prior to agreeing to the purchase. By the way, is this going in one name or two?

Buyer: Both of our names will be on it.

Salesperson: Got it. Can I get the correct spelling of both names, please?

You begin filling in the contract with their names, assuming that they will buy the house. Fill in the entire contract, asking questions about the terms in the contract. We cannot cover the dialogues in detail, because each state's contracts are a bit different.

Salesperson: Let's go over everything that is written.

Questions to Use While Writing a Contract

Here are some questions you would want to ask during the contract-writing time:

- Is there anything in the house that you want to be sure that the homeowner leaves with the house?
- How much would you like to put down as your initial investment?
- Is FHA or conventional financing best for you?
- Would you like to put 10 percent of the sales price as earnest money, or would 5 percent suit you better?
- Would you be willing to pay for the survey, or should we ask the homeowner to pay for it?
- Do you have a home inspector you would prefer, or would you want me to provide you with a list?
- Can you meet the home inspector at the house later this week?
- Is closing within 60 days acceptable to you?
- Would you be willing to allow the homeowner the week-end to move out?
- Did the mortgage company indicate that the homeowner needs to help you with your closing costs?

These questions give you an example of the dialogue you should use during the contract-writing time. Questions give the client permission to be involved and yet enable you to direct the client. Once you've finished writing the contract, you should go back over it with your client to explain what was filled in and get initials and signatures where needed.

Dialogue to Use When Reviewing the Contract

Salesperson: Now that we have completed the paperwork, let's go back over it, can we?

Buyer: Yes, please.

Salesperson: First ...

Salesperson: Any questions on the paperwork?

Buyer: No, I think that covers it.

Salesperson: Great. All I need is your approval right here, and I will do my best to get you happily moved!

Salesperson: Who has the checkbook?

Buyer: I do.

Salesperson: Fine. Make out the earnest deposit check to Acme Title Company and an option fee check to the homeowner, and I'll make you a copy of this agreement. Would you also like a copy of both of your checks?

Buyer: Yes.

Salesperson: Understood. No problem.

Dialogues for Handling Buyer Objections

At times a buyer will want to buy a house but will have objections to making the commitment. The real estate professional can recognize this and overcome those objections. The real estate professional recognizes that objections indicate that the client is interested and that failure to handle them will result in a lost sale. Here are some frequent buyer objections and the dialogues for handling them.

DIALOGUE WHEN THE BUYER IS IN A HURRY

Salesperson: I understand that your time is limited. However, it would be very difficult to properly show that home to you in just 15 minutes. May I suggest we set a time that's convenient for both of us, and perhaps I can arrange other potential homes to show you at the same time? Does that make sense?

DIALOGUE WHEN YOU NEED TO UNDERSELL BAD FEATURES I

Occasionally you will need to undersell a property. The reason you may want to do that is to prepare the buyers. If buyers are prepared for the worst, then the property may not seem as bad to them. They will tend to look for the good.

Salesperson: Mr. and Mrs. Vinson, you're probably not going to like the way this home looks. You may have to replace the carpet, paint, and landscape.

DIALOGUE WHEN YOU NEED TO UNDERSELL BAD FEATURES II

Salesperson: Mr. and Mrs. Vinson, I would like to prepare you for this next home we will look at. It's in pretty bad shape. The potential is there, but you will need to redo the kitchen, including appliances, as well as flooring and paint.

DIALOGUE WHEN YOU NEED TO UNDERSELL BAD FEATURES III

Salesperson: You will need to see this home for what it can become, rather than what it is, because it is a mess currently.

DIALOGUE WHEN THE BEDROOMS ARE TOO SMALL

Salesperson: The builder used the square footage in the primary rooms rather than the secondary rooms.

Dialogues to Use While Showing the Home

DIALOGUE WHEN SHOWING THE HOME I

Salesperson: You mentioned the kitchen was important to you. Why don't we start there, OK?

DIALOGUE WHEN SHOWING THE HOME II

Salesperson: I want you to make yourselves at home. You are welcome to open doors, closets, and cabinets. You will need to get a feel for the entire home, indoors and out. I'm just here to answer your questions. However, there are a few important features of this home. Could I show those to you, if you would let me?

DIALOGUE ABOUT STAYING TOGETHER I

Keep your buyers together. When they separate, personal items in the house could disappear. Even if nothing bad happens, you cannot sell to both unless they are together.

Salesperson: Mr. and Mrs. Vinson, if we can all just stay together, I can point out some of the special features of this home and answer any questions you might have. Can we do that?

DIALOGUE ABOUT STAYING TOGETHER II

Salesperson: Mr. and Mrs. Vinson, it is important that we all stay together as we look at this home and all the homes today. Would you folks stay together, please?

DIALOGUE ABOUT STAYING TOGETHER III

Salesperson: I don't mean to sound rude, but we keep drifting apart as we look at this home. It's better for all us if we stick together as we look through. Let me ask you one more time, could we please stay together?

DIALOGUE ABOUT PERSONAL PROPERTY

Buyer: Is the refrigerator included?

Salesperson: Let me ask you this: if the owner would leave the refrigerator, would you buy this house?

Buyer: I don't know about that, but we would like to have the refrigerator.

Salesperson: Understood. Let me make a note of that.

DIALOGUE ABOUT THE SIZE OF THE HOME

Buyer: How many square feet does this home have?

Salesperson: The tax records indicate 2,850 square feet. Does that seem reasonable?

Buyer: Our current house only has 1,800 square feet, so this home seems huge.

Salesperson: Can't you just imagine how nice it will be to have the room to really live!

DIALOGUE ABOUT A LOWER OFFER

Salesperson: Worst-case scenario, if the owner rejects this offer, you may have to be willing to offer $5,000 or $10,000 more to get it, so let's hope the owner is a little desperate and will accept this offer as written.

DIALOGUE TO USE IF A ROOM IS TOO SMALL

Buyer: I like the home and location, but I hate the fact that this bedroom is too small.

Salesperson: Would you be willing to search for another home with larger rooms if it cost you $15,000 to $20,000 more than this house?

Buyer: Well, no.

Salesperson: Could you live with the room and maybe adjust?

DIALOGUE FOR THE END OF A SHOWING I

Salesperson: Mr. and Mrs. Vinson, now that you've seen this home, how do you feel about it?

Buyer: I liked it all right.

Salesperson: On a scale of 1 to 10, with 10 being the best, what would you rate this home?

Buyer: Maybe a 6.

DIALOGUE FOR THE END OF A SHOWING II

Salesperson: Mr. and Mrs. Vinson, now that you've seen this home, how do you feel about it?

Buyer: I like it better than the first home.

Salesperson: Understood. On a scale of 1 to 10, with 10 being the best, what would you rate this home?

Buyer: Maybe an 8.

Salesperson: Fine. Then can we completely eliminate the first home?

Buyer: Yes.

Salesperson: Would you like to buy this home?

Buyer: No, I would like to look at more.

Chapter 8
Closes and Objection-Handling Dialogues

The term "closing a client" has a negative connotation. The words make us think that what we are doing is against the will of the client. Nothing could be further from the truth. Closing is a natural process that ends a process of discussion and analysis. It is, in its simplest form, asking for a commitment. Closing is what separates the professional salesperson from the order taker. The income of the professional salesperson far exceeds that of an order taker.

The term "objection-handling dialogue" has a mystical meaning. When we hear those words, we think that there is some magical phrase that, if spoken, will overcome any objection that our client can utter. Again, nothing is further from the truth. No objection-handling dialogue will work every time, but any objection-handling dialogue will work some of the time; hence we must have many dialogues to choose from. There is nothing that is magical in using objection-handling dialogues; as a matter of fact, working them is ordinary. The basis of true objection handling is asking questions. The more in-depth the questions, the

Closes and Objection-Handling Dialogues

better and more easily we can handle objections.

This chapter presents and discusses the following:

- Closing dialogues
- Dialogues for overcoming an objection by a buyer
- Dialogues for overcoming an objection by a homeowner

This chapter is intended for practically anyone in the business arena. It is specifically of benefit to real estate salespeople, brokers, managers, attorneys, accountants, and other real estate professionals and to lending professionals, real estate investors, and title officers. All of the above will benefit from knowing the closing dialogues and objection-handling dialogues discussed in this chapter. Without this knowledge, they would be disadvantaged.

These are the objectives of this chapter:

- Understand the reason for using closing dialogues.
- Be able to use closing dialogues in the real estate business.
- Recognize objections from buyers and then handle the objections using dialogues.
- Recognize objections from homeowners and then handle the objections using dialogues.

Closing Dialogues

The art of closing is practiced through asking lots of questions. The "artists" are those real estate professionals who have learned the best dialogues given in this chapter and then use these dialogues with their clients. The clients simply see the beauty of the salesperson's delivery but cannot see the time and practice it took to get there.

The biggest reason other real estate salespeople fail to get the sale is that they get into explanations far too early without asking enough questions. If you say something, then the client will doubt it. If you can get the client to say something through asking questions, it will become absolute truth. The following are closing dialogues with the use of questions.

ALTERNATE CHOICE CLOSE

An alternate choice is a close that only has two answers. Either answer is a minor agreement leading toward the major decision—to purchase.

Salesperson: I am available now. Or would later today be more convenient?

Salesperson: I can be available at six o'clock or eight o'clock. Which would better suit your time schedule?

Salesperson: If everything goes according to your plan, would you like to move in two months, or would three be better?

Give your clients a choice between two actions, not between doing something and not doing it. Alternate choice closes should always be used when setting appointments.

INVOLVEMENT CLOSES

An involvement close is any question you ask buyers that they themselves would ask if they owned the home. Involvement closes make the buyers visualize owning the home.

Salesperson: Would this be your son's or your daughter's room?

Salesperson: Would you place your couch against this wall or over there?

Involvement closes require an answer other than yes or no. Notice that these are very specific and purposeful alternate choice closes.

You can use the involvement close with homeowners. In that case, the questions make the homeowner visualize you marketing the home.

Salesperson: Shall we place the key box on the front door or on the back door?

Salesperson: We can have your house on the property tour this week, or would next week be better for you?

TRIAL CLOSES

A trial close tests the water to see if the buyers are ready to buy a particular house. This is similar to the involvement close, except you can use a trial at any point about anything to test the buyer's interest.

Salesperson: Would you be willing to buy the home if the owner would pay your closing costs?

Salesperson: Would you repaint this room, or would you leave it as is?

The trial close can also be used on homeowners to test whether they are willing to have you market their home.

Salesperson: Would you prefer me to install a stake sign or a post sign?

Salesperson: We could run an advertisement on your property, but we must agree tonight for me to market your home. Would you want it in the next advertisement run?

ISOLATION CLOSE

The isolation close confirms that the objection given is the only one the client has. There's no need to fight objection after objection. If the client has many objections, then pass over the minor ones until you find the major objection.

Salesperson: In addition to the carpet needing replacing, is there any other reason you would not buy this home?

Salesperson: Is that the only thing that is standing in the way of you purchasing this home?

Salesperson: If I am hearing you correctly, if it weren't for the lack of a swimming pool, you would buy this home. Is that correct?

Salesperson: Besides that, is there anything else keeping you from presenting an offer to the homeowner today?

Salesperson: In other words, if it weren't so far from your work, you would like to own this home?

TIE-DOWN CLOSE

A tie-down close is one that ties down a certain point you want to make. The tie-down requires the client to answer, even if just with a nod. This begins to create a yes momentum that is hard for the client to stop.

> *Salesperson:* This room has a lot of character, doesn't it?

The tie-down is "doesn't it?" The client would have to respond. He or she may only nod, but he or she must respond. The tie-down can be used at the end of a sentence, at the beginning, or even in the middle.

> *Salesperson:* Wouldn't it be great seeing your children playing in your own yard?

Tie-downs should only be used to tie down positives. Do not overuse them, or they become annoying. But the more you can make your clients nod, the easier it will be for them to nod yes on your commitment close.

Tie-downs could also be used for homeowners.

> *Salesperson:* A company with a proven track record is important, isn't it?

> *Salesperson:* Don't you agree that an open house on this home would be effective?

ASSUMPTIVE CLOSE

An assumptive close is one in which you assume you have made the sale.

> *Salesperson:* We will have a sign out by Thursday. We will be working together for six months. You will be on the MLS.

The salesperson just assumes that the homeowner will agree to market the property for six months. If you ask, "How long would you like to market the home?" you may be very disappointed by the answer. With an assumptive close, the client must stop you or you are moving on.

> *Salesperson:* I need a check to the title company for $500 earnest money.

Salesperson: I have taken a picture of your house and placed it on a sample advertisement. How do you think it looks?

ASSUMPTIVE TIE-DOWN CLOSE

You can combine closes for a different effect. With an assumptive tie-down, you make an assumptive close that you immediately tie down.

Salesperson: You want to sell your home within three months, don't you?

The assumptive close is "You want to sell your home within three months." The tie-down is "don't you?"

Salesperson: You do want to live in a better neighborhood, isn't that true?

COMPARATIVE CLOSE

The comparative close is designed to enable you to concentrate on something you want to talk about and to dismiss or eliminate something you don't.

Suppose a buyer is concerned that the bedrooms are small.

Salesperson: Isn't it true that the smaller the bedrooms, the more space that can be devoted to the living areas?

All your client has to do is to say yes, and you no longer have to be concerned about the size of the bedrooms. All you talk about now is how much bigger the living room is compared with the living rooms in the other homes you have shown.

A comparative close should always start out with "Isn't it true that ... ?"

Suppose a homeowner is concerned about the commission compared with a reduced commission from another company.

Salesperson: Isn't it true that you get what you pay for?

FEEDBACK CLOSE

When a client states something that is not quite accurate or is of doubtful value as an objection, you use a feedback close. All that is necessary for this close is to take the statement the client has just made and feed it back very nicely as a question.

Homeowner: Your commission is too high.

Salesperson: The commission is too high?

Buyer: This house is too far from my work.

Salesperson: This is too far from your work?

Homeowner: I don't want a sign on the property.

Salesperson: You don't want a sign on the property? Could you elaborate on that?

With a feedback close, you make your client rethink what he or she just said, and this rethinking will demonstrate to him or her the inaccuracy of the statement. Feed back only statements that are in error, or you will reinforce the client's belief.

SANDWICH CLOSE

The sandwich close is a form of questioning that takes a major benefit a client will get and sandwiches it around a minor objection the client is expressing. The emphasis is on the benefit, and the client will see that the objection is not as important.

Used with a buyer:

Salesperson: Mr. and Mrs. Vinson, isn't it true you expressed your need for a good school system for your children (benefit) and this house offers that. Isn't it also true that having to replace the carpet (objection) isn't as important as a quality education for your children (benefit)?

Used with a seller:

Salesperson: Mr. and Mrs. Vinson, I know you have to be out of this house in two months (benefit). I also know that it is important to get the most money possible from the house, but that may mean waiting another six months. Isn't it true that the extra money (objection) is less important than moving before the two months are up (benefit)?

SIMILAR SITUATION CLOSE

In this close you relate a story (which must be true) about someone who was in the same situation as your client. People like to feel that their situation is not unique and that other people have been in the same situation. And the outcome for those people was good, or they figured out how to avoid a bad outcome. This dialogue can be used both with buyers and with sellers.

This dialogue shows a good outcome.

Homeowner: We don't want to paint and replace the carpet.

Salesperson: I understand that it is a hassle and costs some money. I worked with a couple who felt the same way, but I convinced them to do the minor remodeling. After they completed it, the house sold in a shorter time and for more money than the homeowners actually wanted. At closing they thanked me for the advice and said that I possibly earned them thousands of dollars. Now, Mr. and Mrs. Vinson, I advise remodeling only because I want the same results for you. Does that make sense?

The following dialogue shows an outcome that should be avoided:

Buyer: We really like the house but want to think about it until tomorrow.

Salesperson: Yes, you could do that, but I would hate for you to make the same mistake as another couple who were my clients. You see, they said that they wanted to think about it too. I allowed them to do that, and the next day they called me and said they were on their way to my office to write up an offer. I pulled the listing and, to my horror, found that it went pending the night before. I immediately called the listing agent, who told me the homeowner had accepted an offer at 8 p.m. My clients would have submitted their offer by 4 p.m. I can't tell you the pain I had to go through telling the buyers I had cost them their dream home. That's what I did when I let them wait when they should have acted. Now you are asking me to do the same thing. I don't want the same results for you. Please, if you are serious about buying this house, can we at least put an offer to them today?

REDUCE-TO-THE-RIDICULOUS CLOSE

The reduce-to-the-ridiculous close is taking a larger number and spreading it over time to make the number seem smaller.

Salesperson: Let's get this straight. The homeowner wants $100,000, and you are only willing to offer $95,000. Is that correct?

Buyer: That's correct.

Salesperson: In reality, then, we are off by only $5,000. Do you agree?

Buyer: Yes.

Salesperson: How long do you plan on staying in the home?

Buyer: The rest of our lives.

Salesperson: That's great to hear, but if you stay there only the length of the loan, that would be 30 years, right?

Buyer: Right.

Salesperson: That $5,000 over those 30 years works out to be only $160 or so per year. For that $160 you get the over-sized garage to do your woodworking, and you get the gourmet kitchen with the island. It seems a small price to pay to get what you really want. I wonder what that would be per month?

Buyer: I don't know.

Salesperson: Well, let's see, it looks like about $13. Just $13? What does it cost for the two of you to go to the movies?

Buyer: More than $13.

Salesperson: Yeah, and that won't get you popcorn or a soda. Just think, for the price of a movie you get the home of your dreams. I wonder what that would be daily? Let's see. Oh, my gosh—only 40 cents! For 40 cents you get the split bedrooms and the walk-in closets and the formal dining room and an extra study. For less than a cheap cup of cof- fee, you get this home. Of all the homes you've seen, I believe you like this one the most. Are you really going to let 40 cents a day stand in the way of getting this home for you and your family?

Objection-Handling Dialogues—Buyers

An objection is when a buyer feels that there is something wrong with an otherwise suitable property. If you overcome the objection, then the buyer will move forward and buy. (Of course, a buyer may have more than one objection that you must overcome.) Do not misunderstand; the professional real estate salesperson would never attempt to overcome an objection if doing so were not in the best interest of his or her client.

BUYER RELUCTANCE I

Buyer reluctance is when a buyer is interested in a property but is reluctant to make a formal offer. This is a form of stall, and a stall is delaying making a commitment. You may think there is nothing wrong with a client thinking for a couple of days about a purchase, but I can tell you that the first time one of your clients misses out on an opportunity and begins to yell at you, you will change your mind. If an opportunity is right for your client, you are obligated to help him or her make the right decision.

Salesperson: Mr. and Mrs. Vinson, I really believe you two will be happy you made the decision to own this home. We've looked at several homes, and you're most excited about this one. It's in the area where you're looking, and the price is right. I would never recommend a home to you unless I was sure it was right. I live and work in this area, and I want my clients to be on good terms with me in when we run into each other in the future. I do feel this is the right home for you. Could we move forward and present an offer to the homeowner?

Use this dialogue when your clients are hesitating slightly and just need a simple nudge to make the commitment.

BUYER RELUCTANCE II

If your client is very reluctant to make the correct decision, you should use this option.

Buyer: We really want to think it over before making an offer.

Salesperson: I understand that this is a very important decision for you. How long do you think you will need to think it over?

Buyer: It's Friday. Maybe by the end of the weekend.

Salesperson: I see. So Sunday then?

Buyer: Yes.

Salesperson: Do you like the home?

Buyer: Yes, we do. We just want to think it over.

Salesperson: Understood. Is the price OK?'

Buyer: Yeah, not bad.

Salesperson: And the location?

Buyer: It's in the area where we're looking.

Salesperson: That's what I thought. Let's do this, if you agree. Let's place an offer with the homeowners, tying up the property until Sunday. We can do that by using an option. The option gives you the right to terminate the offer for any reason within a certain time frame. By using an option, can we move forward?

Here the real estate salesperson softens the dialogue by leading the clients to believe that they could take a little time to think about the decision. Then the salesperson uses the option to close.

PRICING OBJECTIONS

Buyers are always looking for a good deal. Too many real estate salespeople let the buyers make ridiculously low offers. At times you must help your buyer client offer the market price because the buyer wants the house, and if you fail to help him or her get it, you are not acting like a professional salesperson.

Buyer: Will the owner take less?

Salesperson: All I know is that the owner will take the list price. There is a lot of activity on this property. What were you thinking about offering?

Follow this dialogue up with lots of questions. Understand that if the property is truly overpriced, then you are obligated to inform your client and make the proper offer of market value.

NOT RIGHT TIME TO BUY

Buyers always feel it is not the right time to buy, and yet they always do. I have been in all kinds of markets, and buyers still buy. Sometimes they have to buy smaller houses, but they still buy. This objection is more of a stall than an actual objection. This buyer is just reluctant to make a commitment.

Buyer: I don't feel it is the best time to buy.

Salesperson: Really? Why is that?

Buyer: The real estate market is down.

Salesperson: Wow! That's the reason to buy. Right now buyers will get the best deal maybe of all time. If you wait, you may regret it when you have to pay a considerable amount more. Let's think about it again. Could we buy now?

Buyers think that a down market is a bad time to buy, when in reality it is the best time to buy.

BAD NEIGHBORHOOD

Occasionally, a buyer will object that the neighborhood is bad. Rarely is this actually true, or else you did not do your homework. What I mean is that if you qualified this buyer correctly, he or she is comfortable with the neighborhood. If this is your first showing and the buyer hates the neighborhood, simply state that you understand and take him or her to another neighborhood. Generally, however, we assume that this is a stall and the buyer is simply showing reluctance.

Buyer: I don't like the neighborhood.

Salesperson: We can go to another neighborhood. What is it that you don't like?

Buyer: The other houses are in bad shape.

Salesperson: I understand. Many times we find the home we've always wanted in a neighborhood that's not as nice as we want. In this particular case, are you prepared to pay $5,000 to $10,000 more for the same house in another area?

I can get buyers into any neighborhood as long as they are willing to pay for it. Some buyers want the champagne neighborhood on a beer budget.

TOO FAR FROM SCHOOLS

Handle this in the same way as the preceding objection.

Buyer: The home is too far from the elementary schools.

Salesperson: Really? How far is too far?

Buyer: It is not within walking distance, and I want to walk Junior to school.

Salesperson: I understand. Would you be willing to drive to the local park and then walk the rest of the distance to the school to get the home that you want?

Sometimes a simple suggestion is all it takes to help convince a buyer to make a commitment.

TAXES ARE TOO HIGH

This objection, once again, is a stall. Rarely will the cost of taxes be a barrier to purchasing a home that the buyers truly love. This objection would occur prior to any showing. You would not show buyers properties in the high tax areas if you knew that they could not afford the taxes.

Buyer: The taxes on this property are twice what we used to pay.

Salesperson: I understand. Taxes are high everywhere. What would you be willing to pay in taxes, and would you be willing to locate farther from your work, considering the price of gasoline these days?

This time the salesperson discounts the objection to high taxes by comparing them with the cost of gasoline and drive time.

DISTRESSED PROPERTY

A buyer may say that a property is in bad shape in order to try to negotiate with you, not understanding that you are probably representing him or her. It is best to point out the advantages and then let the buyer make the decision to move forward or to find another property.

Buyer: The property is a dump and would take a fortune to fix up.

Salesperson: We have already discussed that this property is undervalued because of the fix-up possibilities. You mentioned that you could get this property remodeled at a fraction of the cost of retail and you would then have immediate equity. We can look at other properties, but none with the upside potential of this one. Could you get those repairs completed as you said?

The salesperson simply restates the remodeling possibilities previously discussed and then asks a closing question.

HIGH INTEREST RATES

Generally you will get this type of objection during the qualification stage. At that point you should ask lots of questions and then hit your clients with a time problem: they cannot wait for the market to change.

Buyer: The interest rate is too high.

Salesperson: What were you wanting the rate to be?

Buyer: At least two points lower.

Salesperson: How long would you be willing to wait to get a better interest rate?

Buyer: Well, we need a house within two months.

Salesperson: Do you believe the interest rate will drop, given current market conditions? What if it goes up? How about this? To save you from a possibly worse situation, let's place an offer today. If interest rates go down, you then could consider a refinance. Does that make sense?

Always end any objection-handling dialogue with a closing question. You must ask for the commitment each and every time.

Objection-Handling Dialogues—Homeowners

Objection-handling dialogues with homeowners are extremely similar to the dialogues given to handle objections from buyers. Always ask lots of questions, and be patient. Sometimes your clients need to rationalize before making a commitment.

LENGTH OF TIME IN REAL ESTATE I

This is one of my favorite objections, because the new real estate salesperson fears this one above all. Interestingly enough, I got this objection all the time when I was new and have never gotten it as a veteran. The difference was clearly my confidence. As I became better with these dialogues, my clients recognized my professionalism and did not question my time in the business.

Homeowner: How long have you been in the business?

Salesperson: Well, Mr. Vinson, I'm brand new, and that's really an advantage for you. Because I'm new, I have no past successes to rest on. I have to prove myself each and every day. You are one of the most important people in the building of my career, because if I do a good job for you, will you recommend me to your friends?

Homeowner: If you do a good job.

Salesperson: Great! Let me get started today!

Here the salesperson used the "I work hard" close. Always use a closing question.

LENGTH OF TIME IN REAL ESTATE II

My favorite way to handle this one is to get the client to

acknowledge that success is more important than experience and then to use the "if . . . then" close.

Homeowner: How long have you been in the business?

Salesperson: That is an interesting question. Why did you ask me that?

Homeowner: I want to make sure that whoever I hire has the experience to get my house sold.

Salesperson: If I were able to prove to you that I could sell your house, then would you list it with me?

Homeowner: If you could prove it, yes.

Salesperson: Great! Let's look at my marketing plan. . . .

The salesperson clarifies the objection and then uses the if . . . then close. Understand that homeowners do not really care how long you have been in the business as long as they believe that you can sell their home.

I CAN SELL MY HOME WITHOUT USING A REAL ESTATE AGENT

This is the standby threat of homeowners. When homeowners use this line, you must have said something they know is true but did not like. Suppose you showed the homeowners how much they could get for their house and they want more. That's when they decide to make this objection. You must stay firm.

Homeowner: I can sell my home without using a real estate agent. Why do I need you?

Salesperson: Have you thought about how you would market the home?

Homeowner: Well, no, but it can't be that difficult.

Salesperson: Do you have the proper forms to use when you find a potential buyer?

Homeowner: Well, no.

Salesperson: You see, I do a great deal more than finding you a buyer. If I could prove to you that I could save you money and I would still do all the work, would you let me market your home?

Homeowner: Sure.

Now all you have to do is present to the homeowner the value of using you. You are valuable, right? Check your value package, and then demonstrate to the homeowner the value of those services.

NO YARD SIGN I

The "no yard sign" reaction occurs typically with higher-priced homes. Do not fight over this one. If the homeowner will list the house with you for your full listing period, at your full listing commission, and at the correct selling price, list it! Don't fight about the small stuff. The house will be harder to sell without a sign, but it will still sell.

Homeowner: I don't want a yard sign in my front yard.

Salesperson: And why is that?

Homeowner: They are ugly.

Salesperson: I am not sure I understand. Have you seen our yard signs? Because they are designed to attract buyers, not fend them off. Could we agree on a place for the installation to make the yard more appealing?

The salesperson asks a question, overcomes the objection, and finishes with a closing question.

NO YARD SIGN II

Homeowner: I don't want a yard sign.

Salesperson: May I ask why not?

Homeowner: The last time we were selling our home we had a yard sign, and someone broke into our house. I believe the yard sign was a "welcome" sign to the thieves.

Salesperson: Wow, that's terrible! I understand your concern about the sign, but many potential buyers will drive through an area looking for yard signs. We could use a stake sign that you place in the ground while you are at home and pull it up when you leave. Would you be willing to do that?

ADVERTISE MORE I

Homeowner: Will you advertise my house in the newspaper every day?

Salesperson: We will advertise your house to give it the exposure necessary. Only 2 percent of the buyers now come from newspapers. Most of our buyers come from the Internet. Would you like to see our Internet advertising program?

ADVERTISE MORE II

Homeowner: Will you advertise my house in the newspaper every day?

Salesperson: When buyers call in on an ad, they are also calling on your house. You see, if a buyer calls us on an ad for a house down the street from you and figures out that property won't work, we then can tell him or her about your house. So you will be advertised continually, whether your house is actually advertised or not. Does that make sense?

HOLD MORE OPEN HOUSES I

Homeowners believe that open houses are key to selling homes, the same as with advertising. Both can help, but neither will automatically sell a house. One marketing idea does not make a sale, but many will.

Homeowner: Will you hold my house open every weekend until it sells?

Salesperson: Do you actually expect that?

Homeowner: Well, yes.

Salesperson: Has any other real estate professional agreed to that?

Homeowner: Well, no, but I will list with the company that will.

Salesperson: Why do you want your house open every weekend? What do you expect to gain from that?

Homeowner: To get my house sold, that's what!

Salesperson: I see. So if I were to prove to you I could sell your house without holding it open every weekend, then you would list with me?

Homeowner: How could you prove that?

Salesperson: Well, I would have to, but if I could, would you list with me?

Homeowner: Yes, I would.

Salesperson: Great! Now let's look at my marketing plan....

This homeowner is even crazier than most, because he or she wants the house held open every weekend. We could not possibly do that, because we have other clients we must also take care of. The salesperson does not get upset, but continues to ask questions and closes with the "if . . . then" close.

HOLD MORE OPEN HOUSES II

Most homeowners will ask about open houses. If a house meets your criteria for a good open house, you may consider doing one. But no homeowner should expect his or her house to be held open every weekend.

Homeowner: Will you hold my house open every weekend until it sells?

Salesperson: Open houses can generate a flow of buyers through your house, but few actually buy the house they visit. Let's do this. You said you trusted me. Let's allow the customized marketing program 30 days to produce results. Then if it doesn't, we can consider an open house. Is that fair?

This time the salesperson uses the "trust me" close with a follow-up closing question.

HOLD MORE OPEN HOUSES III

Homeowner: Will you hold my house open every weekend until it sells?

Salesperson: Your house is not suitable for an open house. Do you know why?

Homeowner: No. Why?

Salesperson: Because it is at the end of a cul-de-sac street and you get very little drive-by traffic. That's a good thing, because buyers want the privacy, but it makes it less effective for an open house, because no one would come to look. So do you know what we can do?

Homeowner: No.

Salesperson: We can hold open other houses in high-traffic areas that generate a great deal of buyer traffic. The buyers won't like the houses that they are looking at because of the traffic, but we will then take them to your house and sell it. So your house will get the benefit of an open house without the hassle. How does that sound?

Instead of agreeing with the homeowner to do an open house, this salesperson has the courage to respond in a correct manner, but against the wishes of the homeowner. This salesperson says that an open house won't work and then cushions the impact of that response with a question: "Do you know why?" After explaining, the salesperson uses a question to get agreement.

OPEN LISTING

An open listing is one in which a homeowner lists with several brokers and the first to bring a buyer will be the only agent to get paid. This type of agreement is rare, but some homeowners believe that an open listing creates pressure on the brokers to perform. Actually, this is not true, because an exclusive agreement requires performance while an open listing does not. Would you invest much money in marketing a property when you know that you may not be paid?

Homeowner: I will pay you if you bring a buyer, but I don't want to sign any agreement.

Salesperson: Interesting. Why is that?

Homeowner: I want to be flexible to pay whoever sells it.

Salesperson: Oh, I get it. My mistake. You see, I am not being paid to sell your house; I am being paid to get it sold. Do you understand the difference?

Homeowner: Not really.

> *Salesperson:* To get your house sold, I will do whatever it takes. I will give up half of the commission dollars you pay me to do that. If you hire me, I will market it to other real estate salespeople and then pay them just like you would, but I will also do all the marketing for your home to the general public until it sells. Does that sound a lot better than you doing all that?

The salesperson in this dialogue acts like he or she has made the mistake and the homeowner is correct. This reaction makes the homeowner feel good. Then the salesperson takes the conversation a different way and asks a question about the listing agent's function. The salesperson then explains and uses a closing question.

NO KEY BOX

A key box will help the property sell, because real estate salespeople have greater access to the property to show their buyers. The more buyers you get through the house, the better chance to sell.

However, some homeowners believe a key box is a security threat. This is not worth fighting about. If the homeowner is willing to meet the buying agent at the property during showing hours every day of the week, then it should be OK with you. Most homeowners will not do this. Be careful about using this alternative as a close, because the homeowner can turn that around and expect you to meet the buying agents.

> *Homeowner:* I don't want a key box.
> *Salesperson:* And why is that?

Homeowner: I don't like my key being out so anyone can use it.

Salesperson: No doubt! If I were to show you that the key is probably safer in the key box than in your pocket, would you allow me to place it on your front door?

Homeowner: Yes.

Salesperson: I just happen to have one right here. (Shake the key box.) You can hear that there is a key in it. I will give you $5 if you can get that key out in the next minute.

The homeowner frantically digs at the key box.

Salesperson: You see, if I were a burglar, I would have broken your window by now. Do you agree that the key box is safe and secure?

The salesperson in this dialogue allows the homeowner to feel the key box. Sometimes the homeowner needs to be convinced that it is secure. Always finish with a closing question.

INTERVIEWING OTHERS I

Always ask the homeowner if he or she is interviewing others, because you must know if you have competition. Do not bury your head in the sand on this one; be sure to face it head on. Failing to ask may leave you sadly surprised.

Salesperson: Are you talking with any other real estate company about the sale of your house?

Homeowner: I have an appointment with another sales associate from B.S. Realty, Bob Smith's agency.

Salesperson: I don't blame you for that. Are you looking for the best in services for the best price?

Homeowner: Sure.

> *Salesperson:* Great news! I've done your work for you. You
> see, I've shopped our competitors and put together a chart
> of their services and our services. See here. Now, as the
> chart shows, B.S. Realty gives you these services, while we
> give you all those plus all these extras. Mr. and Mrs. Vinson,
> if you could fly first class or coach for the same price, what
> would you do?
>
> *Homeowner:* Fly first class.
>
> *Salesperson:* Exactly! Now hire me and fly first class!

You should have a chart of services, a comparison of what
you offer and what your competitors offer. You can easily
construct this chart using any spreadsheet software. You
must be truthful in your analysis, so you should do some
research. You must also offer more than your competition!
In developing the chart of services, list the services that are
unique to your company. To make the comparison look
valid, include some services that all real estate companies
offer, like MLS. Then present the chart to the homeowner,
and close with a question.

INTERVIEWING OTHERS II

During a listing presentation, you will feel that everything is
going great—and then this pops up.

> *Homeowner:* I have an appointment with a sales associate
> from B.S. Realty, Bob Smith's agency.
>
> *Salesperson:* I don't blame you for that. Is there anything that
> is wrong with my presentation?
>
> *Homeowner:* Oh, no, we just want to be sure.
>
> *Salesperson:* Well, good. I was a bit worried there, because I
> thought we had a connection. But I'm concerned, because

if you are serious about working with me, then having the agent from B.S. Realty come over is a waste of his or her time. I think it might be doing that agent a favor to call and cancel the appointment. In fact, I'd be happy to do it for you. I've received calls like that and really appreciated the respect of my time. Could I go ahead and let the other agent know?

The homeowners may believe they should interview other agents, like getting a second opinion before surgery. This salesperson validates the homeowners' feelings and then turns it around by showing that the homeowners would be wasting the other salesperson's time, which would not be fair. The salesperson then ends with a closing question.

WANTING TO PRICE IT TOO HIGH I

Price is the number-one objection by homeowners. Can you blame them? Every homeowner wants as much for his or her property as possible. Every homeowner believes that his or her property is the best in the area. One major point here: homeowners always know the value of their property. (Maybe not to the penny, but not even real estate professionals would know that.) They know the value assessed for tax purposes, they know what they paid for the property, and they have researched property values in the area.

Homeowner: I want to start at a higher price. I can always come down later if necessary.

Salesperson: That's true. But there are no longer any stupid buyers. Here's what I mean by that. The old standard practice is to price it high and hope to find a buyer who has no idea of the market values. That no longer happens, because all buyers now have computers and the computers can tell them the market values in any area. So the old dialogue is no longer valid: setting the price high may mean losing those smarter buyers. Could we price it right and get it sold to any buyer?

This salesperson uses the old dialogue technique—"This is the way we used to do business, but no longer." Buyers use computers to determine value, so there are no more secrets.

WANTING TO PRICE IT TOO HIGH II

Homeowner: I want to start at a higher price. I can always come down later if necessary.

Salesperson: What do you want to do with this house?

Homeowner: Sell it, of course—but I am not going to give it away.

Salesperson: When you put a house on the market, most of your showings occur within the first 30 days. Do you know why?

Homeowner: Because it is new on the market and generates a lot of activity.

Salesperson: Precisely! Now you want to reduce the price later, when the market has dropped off? If you are willing to lower your price in 30 days, let's lower it now and expose this house to the most potential buyers. Can we do that?

This salesperson shows the homeowner, through the use of questions, that it's better to price the house correctly in the beginning, when there are the most potential buyers available.

WANTING TO PRICE IT TOO HIGH III

Homeowner: The guy over at B.S. Realty said I could get $10,000 more than you are saying.

Salesperson: Did that person show you a detailed, current market analysis for your property?

Homeowner: He did not actually come out with one. I just talked with him on the telephone.

Salesperson: So you feel his analysis of your property is accurate, even though he has never seen the property?

WANTING TO PRICE IT TOO HIGH IV

Homeowner: The guy over at B.S. Realty said I could get $10,000 more than you are saying.

Salesperson: Did that person show you a detailed, current market analysis for your property?

Homeowner: No, not actually, but he did come out to see it, and he felt that it was worth it.

Salesperson: If you call out enough real estate agents, one of them will tell you what you want to hear just to get the listing. I promised that I was going to tell you the truth about what it would take to get your home sold. You told me you wanted me to do that. Put your home on the market at the correct price, and let's get it sold. Can we do that?

Some real estate salespeople will tell a homeowner anything just to get a listing. This is known as buying a listing. The professional real estate salesperson will tell the truth about what it will take to get the property sold, including the truth on pricing.

STALLS AND DELAYS I

A stall or delay is the hesitation prior to making a decision. This is the same for homeowners as buyer reluctance is for buyers.

Homeowner: I want to think it over.

Salesperson: I can understand why you would want to do that. Selling your home is an important decision. Please help me understand. What is it that you need to think about? Is it my company? Do you believe my company can get your house sold?

Homeowner: Yes, you have a fine company.

Salesperson: Is it the marketing plan? Do you believe my marketing plan can get your home sold?

Homeowner: Yes, you have many ways to market my home. It's not that.

Salesperson: Is it me, then? Do you like and trust me?

Homeowner: Of course. I think you are very good.

Salesperson: Is it the price, then? You said you would like to try it at a higher price, but we agreed the correct price in the beginning would be best. So is the price we agreed upon a problem?

Homeowner: Well, yeah, I really need more out of the house.

Salesperson: I see. Let's think this through....

The salesperson uses a series of questions to bring out the hidden objection. The salesperson would then use the appropriate dialogues and finally ask a closing question.

STALLS AND DELAYS II

Homeowner: I want to sleep on it.

> *Salesperson:* Selling your home is an important decision. Just to clarify my own thinking, what is it that you're concerned about? Is it ...?

Then use the preceding dialogue.

REFUSAL TO NEGOTIATE

A homeowner may feel that buyers want to take advantage of him or her. So to counter that, a particular homeowner may stand on a single point and refuse to negotiate.

Homeowner: I won't pay closing costs.

Salesperson: Why is this such a problem?

Homeowner: I paid my own costs, and the buyers of this property can pay theirs!

Salesperson: I see. Remember when we covered your estimated net sheet, what you would make if this house sold for full price?

Homeowner: Yes.

Salesperson: If you net that amount, do you really care how the money above that bottom line is distributed? Let's look at it this way: if a buyer would be willing to pay you more than you are asking for the property, but wanted you to pay the closing costs, would you do it?

Homeowner: Yes, I guess I would.

This salesperson uses the net close and discusses the bottom line instead of concentrating on one term of the deal.

SHORT-TERM LISTING

If a homeowner has sold several houses, he or she might have had a bad experience with a real estate salesperson. Because of that, the homeowner may be hesitant to sign a long-term contract. However, if we don't have adequate time to sell, then we are wasting our time and money.

Homeowner: I only want to give you a 30-day listing.

Salesperson: Interesting. Why is that?

Homeowner: I am not going to lock into a long-term contract and then have you do nothing and tie my property up for six months. If you do a good job, I will relist with you for another 30 days.

Salesperson: It sounds like you've had a bad experience.

Homeowner: You are darn right I did, and I won't make the same mistake again!

Salesperson: I am saddened to hear that. But you see, I am a professional and would not let that happen. Let's take a look at it from this angle. Suppose you own a burger shop. I come in and tell you I'm the best burger flipper you've ever seen. I can flip with both hands and add cheese without breaking a sweat. Then I tell you that I want you to sign a six-month contract to pay me whether I show up and work or not. Would you hire me?

Homeowner: No way!

Salesperson: Isn't that kind of what we do in the real estate profession? We come in here and tell you all the wonderful things we are going to do to get your home sold, and you sign a contract that does not require us to do anything. I am not like that. I will guarantee my services to you: if I don't do what I say I'm going to do, you notify me; and if I don't correct my performance within 10 days, you have the right to fire me. Let me ask you this, Mr. Vinson, if I give you permission to fire me and then I don't perform, will you fire me?

Homeowner: You bet!

Salesperson: I know you would, and that keeps me on my toes and alert because I have never been fired—and I won't be fired now either. Doesn't my guarantee of services make you feel at ease?

This dialogue is structured by a series of questions. The dialogue takes the homeowner outside of real estate and into the burger arena. Sometimes we get too close to real estate to make any sense. The wise salesperson will go outside the industry to make a point. And if you can relate this situation to the homeowner's current work situation, the impact is even greater. The dialogue continues until the salesperson closes with a question.

LOWER COMMISSION I

Homeowner: I want you to lower your commission by 1 percent.

Salesperson: Why?

Homeowner: Because I know commissions are negotiable.

Salesperson: Sure, I agree, but why do you want me to cut my commission?

Homeowner: Uh, because I want to get as much money as possible?

Salesperson: If I could show you how you would net as much, if not more, by paying me a full commission, would you be willing to do that?

Homeowner: Sure.

Salesperson: Great! With all the items on my marketing plan, do you believe it will help you get your home sold faster?

Homeowner: Yes.

Salesperson: And do you agree that the faster your home

sells, the fewer additional house payments you'll be making on it?

Homeowner: Yes.

Salesperson: If you have to make one more house payment because your house didn't sell in a timely manner because you used a commission-cutting agent instead of me, then you've just lost the difference in the commission you are now wanting to save. You get what you pay for! Pay for the best and hire me. Can we get started?

The salesperson uses a series of questions and summarizes with the "if ... then" close. The dialogue continues with explanations until the final closing question.

LOWER COMMISSION II

Homeowner: I want you to lower your commission by 1 percent.

Salesperson: Why?

Homeowner: To save money.

Salesperson: Let's do this instead. Let's raise the price of the house by 1 percent and make me work harder. Would you agree to that?

A 1 percent increase in the sales price is hardly significant, but a 1 percent reduction in your income is huge.

LOWER COMMISSION III

Homeowner: I want you to lower your commission by 1 percent.

Salesperson: Why?

Homeowner: The previous agent I talked with said she would cut her commission by 1 percent.

Salesperson: Let me ask you this: if she was willing to cut her commission that fast, how fast would she cut you on the sales price? You want someone to go into battle for you to protect your money, don't you?

Homeowner: I hadn't thought about it like that.

This exchange is one of the best dialogues, because it mentions taking money out of the homeowner's pocket. Use this one only if the other agent actually cuts his or her commission. An agent can agree to any commission, but if he or she started higher and then cut, the above dialogue is effective.

LOWER COMMISSION IV

Homeowner: I want you to lower your commission by 1 percent.

Salesperson: Hmm. Mr. Vinson, what do you do for a living?

Homeowner: I am a manager for a company that makes automotive parts.

Salesperson: Interesting. Do they pay you for that?

Homeowner: Of course.

Salesperson: What would you do if they cut your salary by over 60 percent?

Homeowner: I would quit.

Salesperson: Interesting that you would quit—and yet that's what you are doing to me.

Homeowner: I am not asking you to reduce your commission by 60 percent. I am only asking you to reduce it by 1 percent.

Salesperson: But I must pay the broker who brings the buyer, and I must pay my broker, and I must pay to get your home sold. All those costs subtract from my income, and then you are cutting it even more. With all that included, you are asking me to cut my income by over 60 percent. Now that you see that, am I really asking that much? Put me to work for you.

This real estate professional is smart enough to bring the discussion out of real estate and into the occupation of the homeowner.

LOWER COMMISSION V

Homeowner: I want you to lower your commission by 1 percent.

Salesperson: Would you be willing to pay all the marketing expenses that I will be willing to pay to get your house sold?

Be careful because this one could cause the homeowner to not like you. Use it only as a last resort, almost as a give-up.

BUY FIRST, THEN SELL

If a homeowner wants to buy before he or she sells, it can be a nightmare for all involved. The timing is off, and pressure is on. Don't let this happen to you or your clients.

Homeowner: We don't want to put our home on the market until we find another one we like.

Salesperson: Interesting. Why would you want to do that?

Homeowner: We don't want to be without a house.

Salesperson: OK, that makes sense. Let me ask you this: if I were to show you how you could end up losing thousands of dollars doing it that way, then would you agree to sell your house first?

Homeowner: Why would I lose money?

Salesperson: I will answer that for sure, but let me ask you again: if I could show you how you could possibly lose thousands of dollars, then would you agree to sell your house first?

Homeowner: Well, I guess I would have to. But why would I lose money?

Salesperson: There are two reasons. First, you must place a contingency on any home you want, stating that you have a house to sell first. To get a homeowner to consider such a contingency, you would have to offer full price or even higher. This alone could cost you thousands. Second, you would then be desperate to get your home sold and would discount the price to enable a quick sale, a move that could also cost you thousands. Now doesn't it make sense to let me do my job and get your home sold and then find you your next home?

During this dialogue, the salesperson uses lots of questions and the "if . . . then" close. The salesperson goes on to prove the point and ends with a closing question.

PERFECT PHRASES
for...

MANAGERS

Perfect Phrases for Managers and Supervisors

Perfect Phrases for Setting Performance Goals

Perfect Phrases for Performance Reviews

Perfect Phrases for Motivating and Rewarding Employees

Perfect Phrases for Documenting Employee Performance Problems

Perfect Phrases for Business Proposals and Business Plans

Perfect Phrases for Customer Service

Perfect Phrases for Executive Presentations

Perfect Phrases for Business Letters

Perfect Phrases for the Sales Call

Perfect Phrases for Perfect Hiring

Perfect Phrases for Building Strong Teams

Perfect Phrases for Dealing with Difficult People

YOUR CAREER

Perfect Phrases for the Perfect Interview

Perfect Phrases for Resumes

Perfect Phrases for Negotiating Salary & Job Offers

Perfect Phrases for Cover Letters

Learn more.  Do more.

Visit mhprofessional.com/perfectphrases for a complete product listing.